TEST YOUR IQ

TEST YOUR IQ

400 new tests to boost your brainpower!

TOP UK MENSA PUZZLE EDITORS
KEN RUSSELL & PHILIP CARTER

KOGAN
PAGE

First published in 2000

Reprinted 2001

Kogan Page Limited
120 Pentonville Road
London N1 9JN
UK

Kogan Page Limited
22 Broad Street
Milford CT 06460
USA

British Library Cataloguing in Publication Data

A CIP record for this book is available from the British Library.

ISBN 0 7494 3299 3

Typeset by Saxon Graphics Ltd
Printed and bound in Great Britain by Biddles Ltd,
www.biddles.co.uk

Contents

Introduction

Intelligence is the ability to respond adaptively to new situations, to think abstractly and to comprehend complex ideas. IQ is the abbreviation for Intelligence Quotient. The word quotient means the number of times that one number will divide into another. An intelligence test (IQ Test) is a standardized test designed to measure human intelligence as distinct from attainments.

The measured IQ of children is equal to mental age divided by actual (chronological) age. For example, if a child of eight years of age obtains a score expected of a ten-year-old, the child will have a measured IQ of 125, by means of the following calculation:

$$\frac{\text{Mental age}}{\text{Chronological age}} \times 100 = \text{IQ}$$

or

$$\frac{10}{8} \times 100 = 125 \text{ IQ}$$

This method of calculating IQ does not apply to adults because beyond the age of 18 there is little or no improvement in mental development. Adults, therefore, have to be judged on an IQ test in which the average score is 100. The results are graded above and below this norm according to known test scores.

The tests that have been compiled for this book have not been standardized, so an actual IQ assessment cannot be given. However, at the end of this Introduction there is a guide to assessing your performance in each test and also a cumulative guide for your overall performance on all ten tests.

The tests are intended as valuable practice for readers who may have to take an IQ test in the future, and they will also help to increase your vocabulary and to develop your powers of calculation and logical reasoning. The questions are challenging, and deliberately so, as this is the only way to boost your performance and increase your brainpower.

The book consists of ten separate tests for you to attempt, each of 40 questions. Each test is of approximately the same degree of difficulty. A time limit of **90 minutes** is allowed for each test. The correct answers are given at the end of the book, and you should award yourself one point for each correct answer.

Use the following tables to assess your performance:

One test

Score	Rating
36–40	Exceptional
31–35	Excellent
25–30	Very good
19–24	Good
14–18	Average

Ten tests

Score	Rating
351–400	Exceptional
301–350	Excellent
241–300	Very good
181–240	Good
140–180	Average

Test one

1   Create two words using the following ten letters each
    once only.

    Clue: grand tune (4, 6)

    MYSEVODLTA

2   Which is the odd one out?

    ISTHMUS, FJORD, ATOLL, POLDER, ARCHIPELAGO

3   What number should replace the question mark?

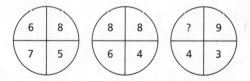

4   CARTON, ENJOYMENT, WORDSMITH
    Which of the following words continues the above
    sequence?

    COPY, REEF, COPE, REST, ACHE

5   Comparison

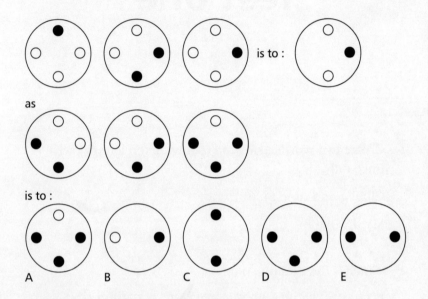

6   What word in brackets means the same as the word in capitals?

FORTE (endowment, conduct, talent, redoubt, style)

7   What number comes next in this sequence?

25, 32, 27, 36, ?

8 Place two letters in each bracket so that these finish the word on the left and start the word on the right. The letters in the brackets, read downwards in pairs, will spell out a six-letter word.

Clue: blue-pencil

FA (. .) SK
HO (. .) AN
KI (. .) AR

9 A car travels at a speed of 40 mph over a certain distance and then returns over the same distance at a speed of 60 mph. What is the average speed for the total journey?

10 Spiral clockwise round the perimeter to spell out a nine-letter word, which must finish in the centre square. The word commences at one of the corner squares. You must provide the missing letters.

	N	
B	E	A
A	C	N

11 MEANDER: WIND
     TRAVERSE: a) stampede
                b) forward
                c) across
                d) retrace
                e) towards

12 What familiar phrase is indicated below?

PAGE
PAGE

13 Comparison

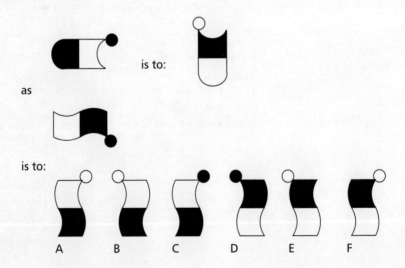

14 The following is an anti-magic square, where none of the horizontal, vertical or corner-to-corner lines totals 34. It is possible, however, by moving the position of just four of the numbers to convert this into a true magic square, where each horizontal, vertical and corner-to-corner line adds up to 34.

Can you make the necessary corrections?

4	14	8	1
9	16	6	12
5	11	10	15
7	2	3	13

15 What do the following words have in common?

LEGUMES, QUASHED, AFFIRMS, CLOAKED

16 What number should replace the question mark?

926 : 24
799 : 72
956 : ?

17 Solve the three anagrams to complete a quotation by Confucius.

Clue: Save something for a rainy day.

WHEN   P . . .P . . . . .   C . . . ., . . N . .
            ↑SOPPY TRIER↑   ↑DEMON COOTS↑

. . E A . . . .   IT.
↑ FOUL ALES ↑

18 Add one letter, not necessarily the same letter, to each word at the front, end or middle to find two words that are opposite in meaning.

LOG PITY

19 What number should replace the question mark?

7	10	9	6
5	1	3	7
2	3	2	1
4	12	8	?

20 What well-known proverb is opposite in meaning to the one below?

Beware of Greeks bearing gifts.

21 Which word means the same as ANCHORITE?

    a) recluse
    b) hieroglyphics
    c) trammel
    d) lackey

22 What is the value of x?

$64 - 12 \times 2 + 6 \div 3 = x$

23 Fill in the blanks, clockwise or anti-clockwise, to form two words that are synonyms.

24 What is JULIENNE?

    a) reed bunting
    b) an evergreen shrub
    c) a sleeveless jacket
    d) clear soup
    e) a skull-cap

25 Grid

Each of the nine squares in the grid marked 1A to 3C should incorporate all the lines and symbols that are shown in the squares of the same letter and number immediately above and to the left. For example, 2B should incorporate all the lines and symbols that are in 2 and B.

One of the squares is incorrect. Which one is it?

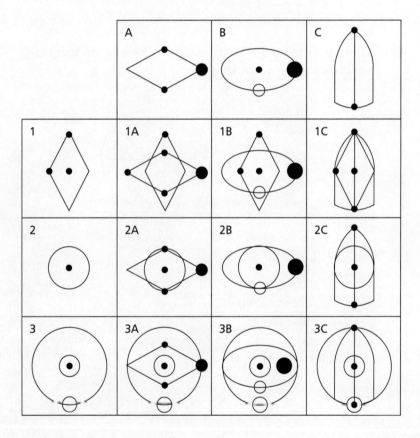

26 Solve the one-word anagram.

APE COLT

27 Insert a word that means the same as the words outside the brackets.

COOK (. . . . .) CROSS EXAMINE

28 What number should replace the question mark?

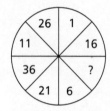

29 Make a six-letter word using only these four letters:

R E
F L

30 Circles

Which of A, B, C, D or E fits into the blank circle to carry on a logical sequence?

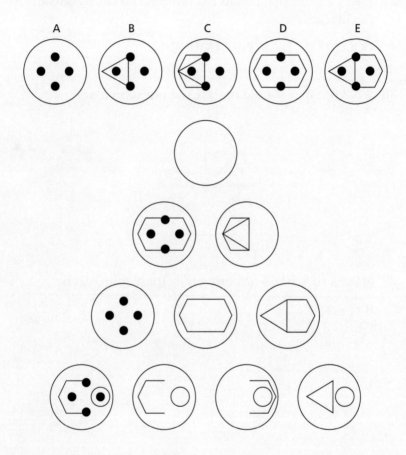

31 Which two words mean the opposite?

DOLOROUS, CONVENE, DISPARAGE, OFFEND, PRAISE, TREMBLE

32 What is the name given to a group of ROOKS?

    a) murmuration
    b) park
    c) building
    d) set
    e) business

33 Replace the dots with a word to make five new words.

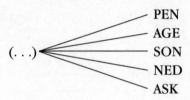

                          PEN
                          AGE
(. . .)   SON
                          NED
                          ASK

34 What number should replace the x ?

$$\frac{5}{6} \div \frac{1}{7} = x$$

35 Hexagon

Which hexagon, A, B, C, D or E, fits the missing space?

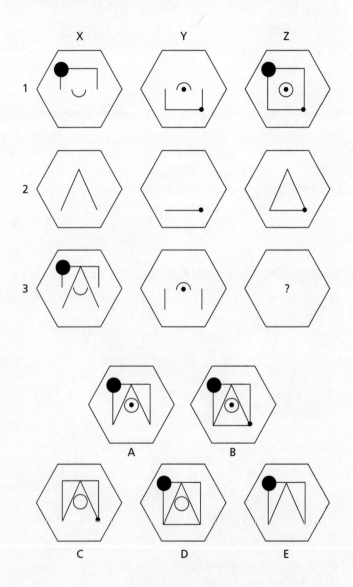

36 Place three two-letter bits together to make a CURRENCY.

   DO – RO – LI – ES – EK – SH – UB – CU – AL

37 What is always associated with a BINNACLE?

   a) a jib
   b) a life raft
   c) a limpet
   d) a mast
   e) a compass

38 Fill in the blanks, clockwise or anti-clockwise, to
   complete the word.

39 What number should replace the question mark ?

7	8	8	48
9	7	5	58
11	5	7	48
6	12	5	?

40 Symbols

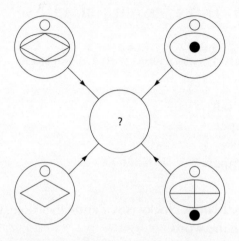

Each line and symbol that appears in the four outer circles, above, is transferred to the centre circle according to these rules:

if a line or symbol occurs in the outer circles:

once:	it is transferred
twice:	it is possibly transferred
3 times:	it is transferred
4 times:	it is not transferred.

Which of the circles A, B, C, D or E, shown below, should appear at the centre of the diagram, above?

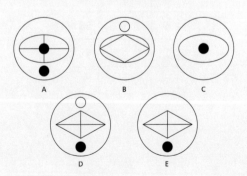

Test two

1   How many lines appear below?

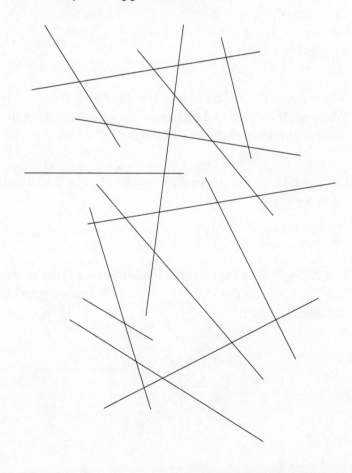

2   Susceptible to attack or damage.

Which word below most closely fits the above definition?

DEBILITATED, VULNERABLE, UNSTABLE,
EMASCULATED, UNPREPARED

3   SUNDAY
    MONDAY
    TUESDAY
    WEDNESDAY
    THURSDAY
    FRIDAY
    SATURDAY
    SUNDAY

Which day is three days before the day immediately
following the day two days before the day three days after
the day immediately before Friday?

4   Change one letter only in each word below to find a well-
    known phrase.

    ON TIE WINK

5   Spiral clockwise to spell out a ten-letter word that starts
    and finishes with the same two letters. You must provide
    the missing letter.

6   Insert the letters provided into the spaces to spell out a
    palindromic phrase, that is, one that reads the same back-
    wards and forwards.

    Clue: exercise franchise

    TREE VISITOR

    . . S . . . . . O . . . . . .

7   Squares

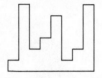

    Which of the following pieces, when fitted to the above
    piece, will form a perfect square?

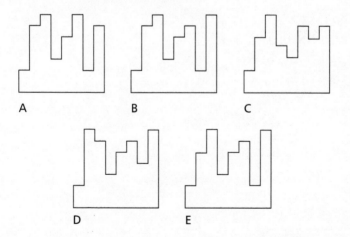

8 On glancing through your morning newspaper you notice that four pages are missing. One of the missing pages is page 8. The back page of the newspaper is 28. What are the other three missing pages?

9 Which of the following is not an anagram of a type of book?

NEIL COX
ASSURE HUT
SUMO BIN
SACK OBOE
ROY COKE

10 Which word in brackets is opposite in meaning to the word in capitals?

SIGNIFICANT (ordinary, stupid, modest, petty, dull)

11 FELINE: CAT
   VULPINE: a) ferret
             b) fox
             c) deer
             d) wolf
             e) sheep

12 What number should replace the question mark?

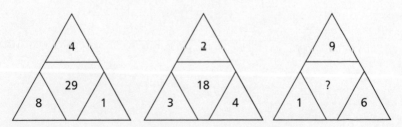

13 Find two words, one in the first grid and one in the
    second, that are antonyms. The words can be read back-
    wards, forwards, horizontally, vertically or diagonally, but
    always in a straight line.

T	E	D	Y	T
R	R	U	L	S
Y	A	A	P	A
S	H	R	P	L
T	S	F	A	B

H	I	M	S	P
P	R	P	M	A
A	A	A	T	S
T	R	A	T	S
T	E	M	A	S

14 Odd one out

Which of A, B, C, D or E is the odd one out?

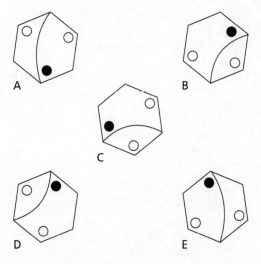

15 Arrange the following words in a line so that each pair of words in the line forms a new word or phrase:

for example: word, game, pass, point = pass, word, game, point to give the words or phrases, password, word game and game-point.

SHORT, GROUP, WATER, LINE, STORY, AGE, FRESH, FALL

16 Which two numbers come next in this sequence?

38, 24, 62, 12, 74, ?

17 Which is the odd one out?

ROOSTER, BUCK, GANDER, PEN, RAM

18 The following is extracted from which hyphenated word?

Clue: viewing area

. . . . . R E – G A . . . . .

19 Which two numbers should replace the question marks?

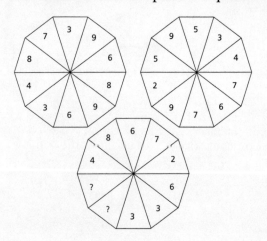

20 OUTLINE TAX is an anagram of which 10-letter word?

21 Fill in the blanks, clockwise or anti-clockwise, to complete the word.

22 What is always associated with a CARBOY?

a) velveteen
b) a mechanic
c) a valet
d) basketwork
e) a bell boy

23 Insert a word that means the same as the words outside the brackets.

SMALL WATCH (. . .) FOIST

24 Solve the one-word anagram.

COD COILER

25 Odd one out

Which of these is the odd one out?

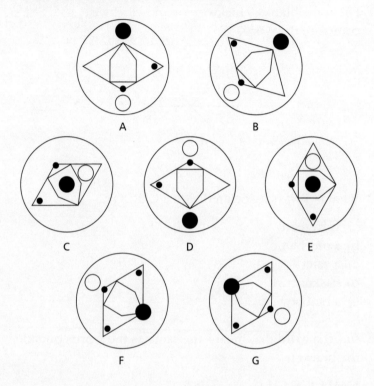

26 What number should replace the question mark?

61, 54, 62, ?, 63, 56, 64

27 What is a KIBITZER?

a) a settlement
b) a covered wagon
c) a trinket
d) a fish trap
e) an onlooker

28 Place two three-letter bits together to make a tree.

CAS – CHE – ACA – RRI – HER – CIA – AND – ALM

29 Replace the dots with a word to make five new words.

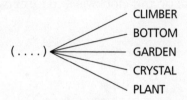

(. . . .)   CLIMBER
              BOTTOM
              GARDEN
              CRYSTAL
              PLANT

30 Circles

Which of A, B, C, D or E fits into the blank circle to carry on a logical sequence?

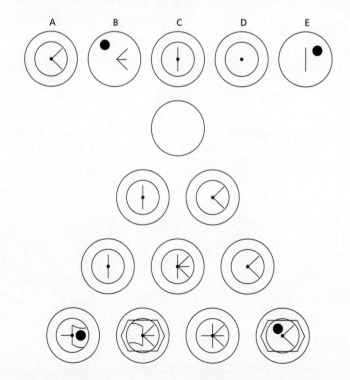

31 Which two words mean the same?

FLACCID, FLICKERING, MENDACIOUS, INFLUENTIAL,
VITAL, LAMBENT

32 Fill in the blanks, clockwise or anti-clockwise, to form two
words that are synonyms.

33 Which word means the same as NEOPHYTE?

a) scallywag
b) junta
c) gimrack
d) novice

34 What is the value of x?

$$\frac{4}{13} \div \frac{9}{52} = x$$

35 Hexagon

Which hexagon, A, B, C, D or E, fits the missing space?

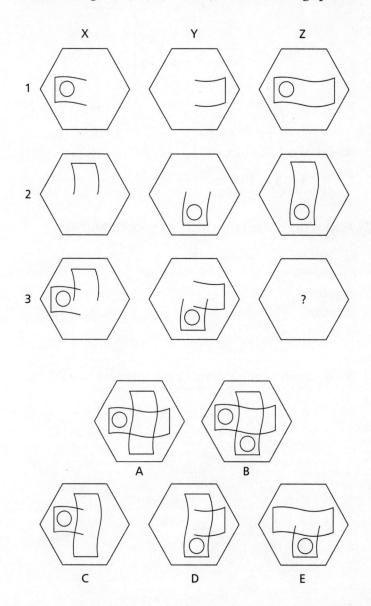

36 What number should replace the question mark?

7	6	4	52
9	3	5	60
10	5	4	60
8	7	3	?

37 What is the value of x?

$7 \times 9 - 3 \times 4 + 10 = x$

38 What is the name given to a group of HERRINGS?

a) caste
b) quiver
c) sute
d) sedge
e) glean

39 What number should replace the question mark?

40 Grid

Each of the nine squares in the grid marked 1A to 3C
should incorporate all the lines and symbols that are
shown in the squares of the same letter and number
immediately above and to the left. For example, 2B
should incorporate all the lines and symbols that are in 2
and B.

One of the squares is incorrect. Which one is it?

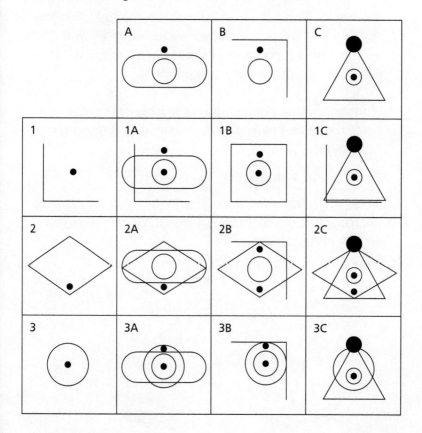

Test three

1 You are looking for one word in this paragraph. The word appears only once, its first letter is the ninth letter to appear after a certain vowel and the same vowel is the fifth letter to appear after its last letter.

2 Find the starting point and track from letter to letter along the lines to spell out the name of an American city (12 letters).

There is one double letter in the name.

Note: when travelling from letter to letter along a side of the triangle, lines may have to pass through letters that are not part of the solution.

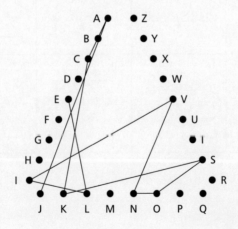

3   Sequence

Which option below continues the above sequence?

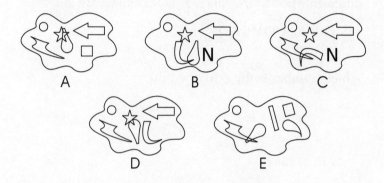

4   What numbers should replace the question marks?

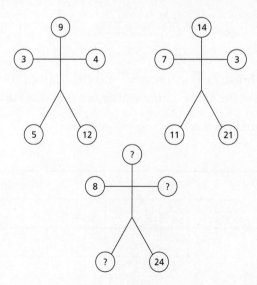

5 Taking the respective numerical position of the alphabet, decode the following phrase, for example IQ TEST = 9, 17, 20, 5, 19, 20 or 9172051920.

1211241211471925145

6 Solve each anagram to find two phrases that are spelt differently but sound alike, as in: 'a name', 'an aim'.

SEMI ARC   CRIME ACE

7 Which number is the odd one out?

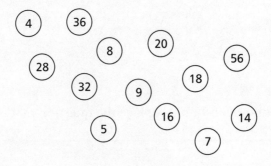

8 What phrase can be inserted into the bottom row to complete the three-letter words reading downwards?

Clue: musical solo

A	F	H	D	L	P	H	P	M	W
G	A	U	I	E	A	O	E	A	A

9 Solve the cryptic clue below. The answer is a 10-letter
   word anagram contained within the clue.

   NEEDLEWORK
   DECORATES
   MY DIRE
   ROBE

10 What is a BURGEE a type of?

   a) elastic
   b) flag
   c) rope
   d) window
   e) food

11 Odd one out

Which is the odd one out?

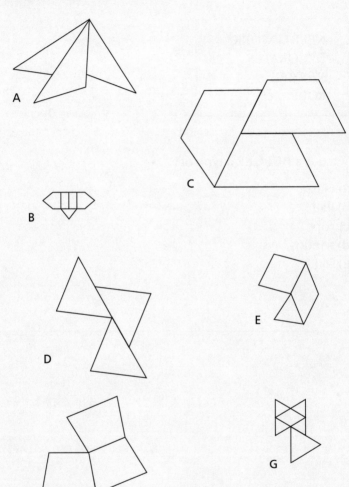

12 Which two of these words are closest in meaning?

GLUT, SUPPLICATION, AID, CACHE, GUIDANCE, PLEA

13 Which number comes next in this sequence?

1, 2, 0, 3, −1, 4, ?

14 Complete each seven-letter word in such a way that the name of a novel is spelt out by the three letters inserted in each word. You are actually looking for seven three-letter words.

HO . . . AD
SC . . . ED
RO . . . CE
SL . . . ER
DI . . . RY
RO . . . TE

15 What, with reference to this question, is the next number in the sequence below?

3, 3, 5, 1, 3, 4, 1, 2, 3, 4, 1, 2, ?

16 Sequence

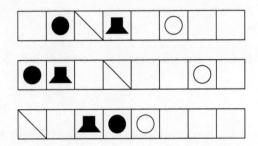

Which option below continues the above sequence?

A

B

C

D

E

17 LOB is to ORE
as ORB is to ?

18

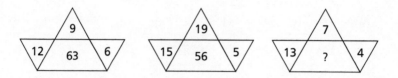

What number should replace the question mark?

19 Which two words that sound alike, but are spelt differently, mean:

SLACK/REQUIRES

20 Which word in brackets is opposite in meaning to the word in capitals?

FREQUENT (glow, restrain, avoid, discard, resort)

21 Fill in the blanks, clockwise or anti-clockwise, to complete the word.

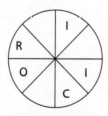

22 What number should replace the question mark?

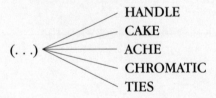

23 What is always associated with DOLMEN?

a) clothes
b) ironwork
c) stone
d) a statue
e) brickwork

24 Replace the dots with a word to make five new words.

(. . .) <
HANDLE
CAKE
ACHE
CHROMATIC
TIES

25 Symbols

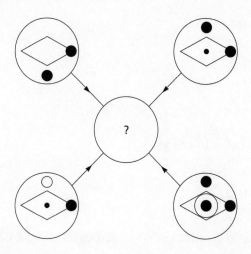

Each line and symbol that appears in the four outer circles, above, is transferred to the centre circle according to these rules:

if a line or symbol occurs in the outer circles:

once:	it is transferred
twice:	it is possibly transferred
3 times:	it is transferred
4 times:	it is not transferred.

Which of the circles A, B, C, D or E, shown below, should appear at the centre of the diagram, above?

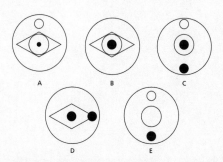

26 What is the name given to a group of FINCHES?

   a) a charm
   b) a cluster
   c) a nest
   d) a pace
   e) a spring

27 What is the value of x?

$$\frac{5}{11} \div \frac{15}{44} = x$$

28 Place three two-letter bits together to make a BIRD.

   CA – NA – AN – GP – GE – IE – RI – MA – PI

29 Make a six-letter word using only these four letters.

   Z G
   F I

30 Comparison

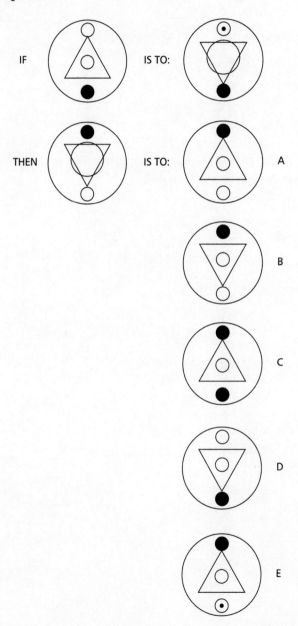

31 Insert a word which means the same as the words outside the brackets.

FROZEN RAIN (. . . .) SUMMON

32 What is the value of x?

$-8 + 6 \times 8 - 2 \times 5 = x$

33 Fill in the blanks, clockwise or anti-clockwise, to form two words which are synonyms.

34 What is a GOOGOL?

a) a mathematical term
b) an albatross
c) a folk dance
d) a carrion crow
e) not a gypsy

35 Grid

Each of the nine squares in the grid marked 1A to 3C should incorporate all the lines and symbols that are shown in the squares of the same letter and number immediately above and to the left. For example, 2B should incorporate all the lines and symbols that are in 2 and B.

One of the squares is incorrect. Which one is it?

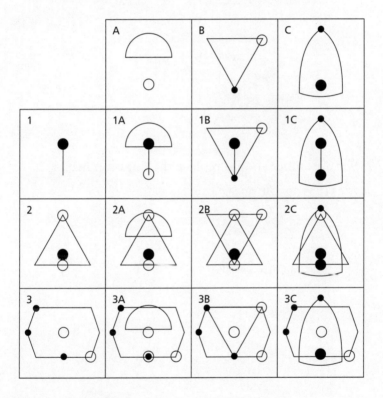

36 Which two words mean the same?

PRETENSION, INDECOROUS, GRATUITOUS, FREE, OVERSHADOW, NEFARIOUS

37 Solve the one-word anagram.

GORILLA SAT

38 What number should equal the question mark?

4	2	8	16
6	3	7	14
9	3	84	24
8	4	16	?

39 What number should replace the question mark?

27, 31, 2, 32, 29, 33, 30

40 Hexagon

Which hexagon fits the missing space?

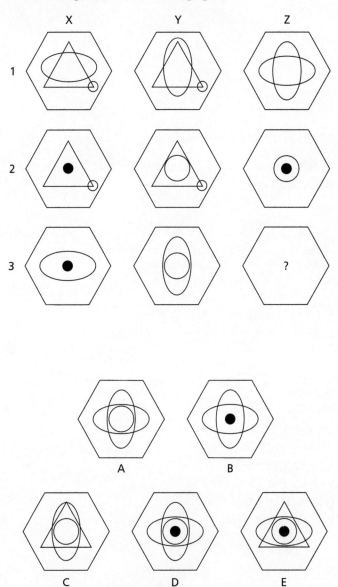

Test four

1 Which is the odd one out?

CLAVICHORD, SPINET, HARPSICHORD, CLARION, ACCORDION

2 'SLOW OR FAST ROADS' is an anagram of which familiar phrase: 2, 1, 4, 3, 5, which means the opposite of verbose?

3 586321 is to 268
as 94783219647 is to ?

4 What do the following have in common?

RHAPSODY IN BLUE
QUICK ON THE DRAW
BOXING MATCHES
WHISKY GALORE
VENUS FLYTRAP
QUESTION MARK
PANTY GIRDLES

5   Shields

Which shield should replace the question mark?

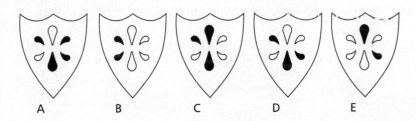

6   Spiral clockwise round one of the circles and anti-clockwise round the other to find two words that have similar meanings.

7   LATTICE : WINDOW

Which two words below have the same relationship as the two words above?

a) portal : gable
b) embrasure : chimney
c) mansard : roof
d) parapet : door
e) fascia : floor

8   Which word in brackets means the same as the word in capitals?

INDISCRETION (crudity, sloth, folly, aversion, vacillation)

9 What numbers should replace the question marks?

7	5	4	6
5	8	10	8
6	?	?	7
8	6	7	9

10 What do the following words have in common?

PRECIOUS, CIRCLE, TONE, AUTOMATIC

11 A well-known phrase has had all its vowels removed and has been split into groups of three letters, which are in the correct order. What is the phrase?

KPT HBL LRL LNG

12 What is the missing number?

2	7	6	8	4
1	2	1	9	6
2	5	4	7	8
6	5	3	5	?

13 What comes next?

A, 1A, 111A, 311A, ?

14 Complete two magic word squares where the same four
words in each square can be read both vertically and horizontally. Clues are given, but in no particular order.

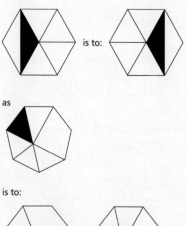

Clues:
1. Dense plant
2. Yard or street
3. Stretch of land
4. Moist
5. Someone in addition
6. Figure of worship

15 Comparison

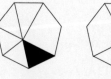

16 Which is the odd one out?

SALIFEROUS, EVACUATION, REGULATION,
EXHAUSTION, INOCULATED, DUODECIMAL

17 Which number is the odd one out?

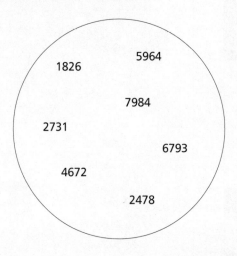

18 Which two words are most opposite in meaning?

MALICIOUS, KNAVISH, HOPEFUL, SERVILE, PRINCIPLED,
AWKWARD

19 Which other 12-letter weather phrase can be placed in the right-hand column in order to complete the three-letter words reading across?

H	A	
I	■	
G	■	
H	E	
P	A	
R	U	
E	A	
S	■	
S	I	
U	■	
R	■	
E	L	

(7, 5)

20 I strode to Dorset, ate milk and rice in Limerick and bought Edna a beer in Aberdeen. Whom did I meet in Antrim?

21 Insert a word that means the same as the words outside the brackets.

SKIN (. . . .) CONCEAL

22 Replace the dots with a word to make five new words.

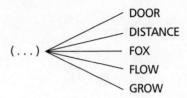

(. . .)
- DOOR
- DISTANCE
- FOX
- FLOW
- GROW

23 Which number should replace the question mark?

24 What is the name given to a group of HORSES?

a) husk
b) haras
c) mute
d) rush
e) sord

25 Comparison

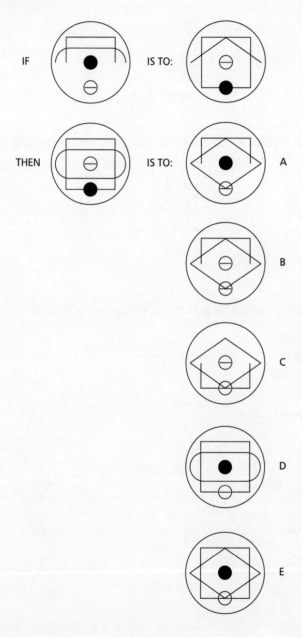

26 Fill in the blanks, clockwise or anti-clockwise, to form two
words that are synonyms.

27 What is an ORRERY?

  a) a clockwork model
  b) a Florentine iris
  c) a golden ornament
  d) a museum
  e) a dungeon

28 What is the value of x?

$$\frac{17}{19} \div \frac{3}{38} = x$$

29 Which one of these is not an animal?

  LAWSEE
  GADBER
  DIHRAS
  MACYAN
  ROUGAC

30 Hexagon

Which hexagon, A, B, C, D or E, fits the missing space?

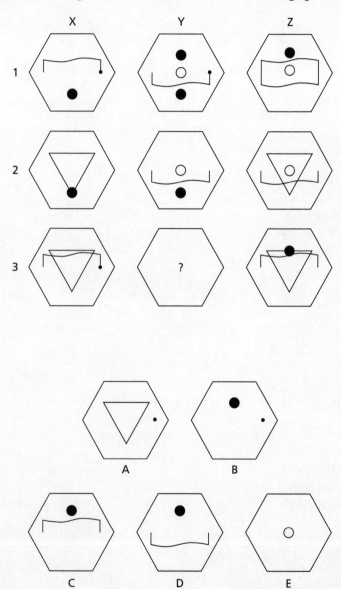

31 What number should replace the question mark?

16		3
	72	
3		4

17		8
	160	
2		1

14		8
	?	
4		3

32 Solve the one-word anagram.

NO MORE STARS

33 Which two words mean the same?

ADVOCATE, LAMPOON, MEDIATE, DEFAME, PROJECT,
ARBITRATE

34 Replace the dots with a word to make five new words.

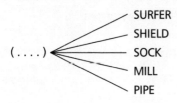

(. . . .) — SURFER
            — SHIELD
            — SOCK
            — MILL
            — PIPE

35 Symbols

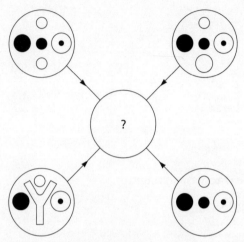

Each line and symbol that appears in the four outer circles, above, is transferred to the centre circle according to these rules:

if a line or symbol occurs in the outer circles:

once:	it is transferred
twice:	it is possibly transferred
3 times:	it is transferred
4 times:	it is not transferred

Which of the circles A, B, C, D or E, shown below, should appear at the centre of the diagram, above?

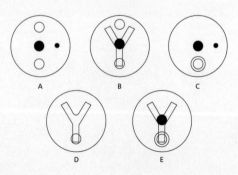

36 What is a HARBINGER?

   a) a flowering shrub
   b) a type of boat
   c) a messenger
   d) a cloak
   e) a drink

37 Fill in the blanks, clockwise or anti-clockwise, to
    complete the words.

38 What is the value of x?

   $3 - 6 \times 7 + 6 \div 4 = x$

39 Place three two-letter bits together to make an ANIMAL.

   EY – CK – DO – AT – RR – ES – NK – FE – JA

40 Grid

Each of the nine squares in the grid marked 1A to 3C should incorporate all the lines and symbols that are shown in the squares of the same letter and number immediately above and to the left. For example, 2B should incorporate all the lines and symbols that are in 2 and B.

One of the squares is incorrect. Which one is it?

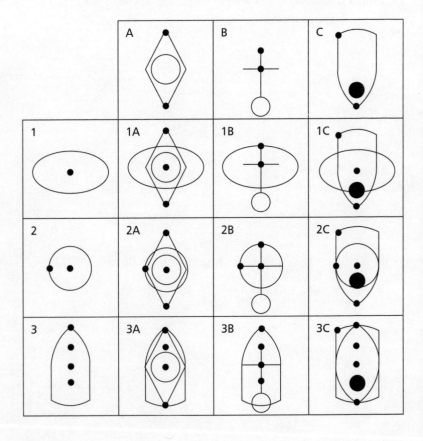

Test five

1 How many circles appear below?

2   Complete the six words so that two letters are common
    to each word. That is, reading across, the same two letters
    that end the first word also start the second word, etc.
    The two letters that end the sixth word are also the first
    two letters of the first word, to complete the circle.

    . . A B . .
    . . N G . .
    . . I E . .
    . . N D . .
    . . A C . .
    . . S S . .

3   You have accidentally left the plug out of the bath and are
    attempting to fill the bath with both taps full on. The hot
    tap takes three minutes to fill the bath and the cold tap two
    minutes, and the water empties through the plug hole in
    six minutes. In how many minutes will the bath be filled?

4   Sequence

What continues the above sequence?

A   B   C   D   E

5   Which word is the odd one out?

AGE   FED
STRIPED   ERA   TAP
THRIFTY
HIT   ASTOUND
TIE
USE   SON
OFFENDS   LAUGHED
RETREAT   GUESSED

6   What number should replace the question mark?

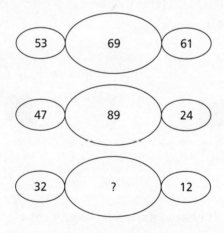

53   69   61

47   89   24

32   ?   12

7   What do these words have in common?

ABUNDANCE, ALLEVIATE, UNTRUTHS, PROCAINE,
CHAMBER

8 What letter should replace the question mark?

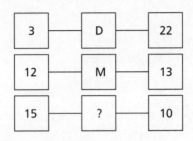

9 Solve the anagram in brackets to complete the quotation correctly. You are looking for a two-word answer (5, 6).

Clue: convenience

The (FUTILE SLOTH) is the basis of western civilization (Alan Coult).

10 Sequence

What comes next in the above sequence?

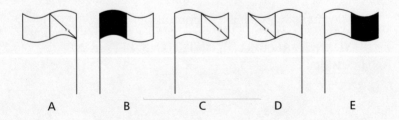

A   B   C   D   E

11 Insert the numbers 1–5 in the circles so that for any
    particular circle the sum of numbers in the circles
    connected directly to it equals the value corresponding to
    the number in that circle, as given in the list.

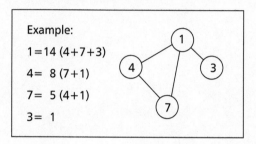

Example:

1 = 14 (4+7+3)

4 = 8 (7+1)

7 = 5 (4+1)

3 = 1

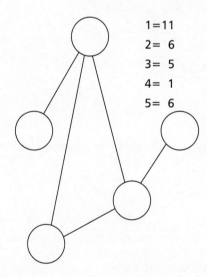

1 = 11

2 = 6

3 = 5

4 = 1

5 = 6

12 Pick a letter from each circle and, reading anti-clockwise, spell out two words that are synonyms. Each word starts in a different circle.

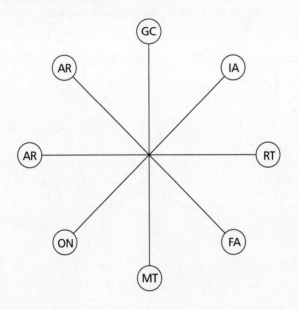

13 Create two words using the following ten letters each once only:

Clue: easier tariff

MXERPLAITS

14 MUSIC: COMPOSE
   DEVICE: a) use
              b) create
              c) construct
              d) invent
              e) change

15 Find two of the three words that will form an anagram synonymous with the word remaining.

Example: LEG – MEEK – NET = MEEK – GENTLE (LEG, NET)

TRUCE – NONE – MEET

16 What number continues this sequence?

987, 251, 369, 872, 513, ?

17 Move horizontally and vertically, but not diagonally, to spell out a 12-letter word. You must provide the missing letters.

E	F	O	
S	O	N	P
	I	A	L

18 What comes next in this sequence?

7, 8, 9, 10, 12, 14, 16, 20, 21, 28, ?

19 Which two words are closest in meaning?

EXPLORER, VAGRANT, MINSTREL, RESIDENT, SOLDIER, ITINERANT

20 Change one letter only from each word to find a familiar phrase:

OUT OF IRE

21 Which one of these is not a vegetable?

ROCART
EYECLR
ROMRAW
TOPAOT
XESTTE

22 What number should replace the question mark?

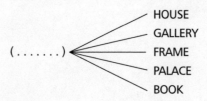

23 Replace the dots with a word to make five new words.

(. . . . . . .)
HOUSE
GALLERY
FRAME
PALACE
BOOK

24 What is the name given to a group of BUTLERS?

a) blast
b) host
c) draught
d) morbidity
e) staff

25 Circles

Which of A, B, C, D or E fits into the blank circle to carry on a logical sequence?

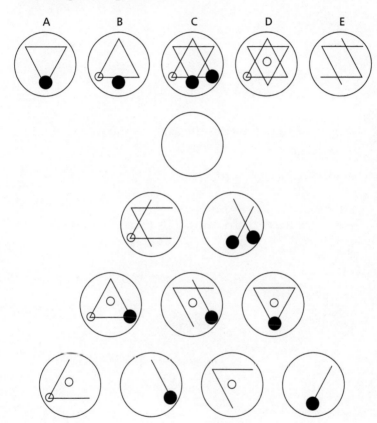

26 What is a CURRICLE?

    a) a vehicle
    b) a boat
    c) a curtain
    d) French dressing
    e) a vegetable

27 Fill in the blanks to complete the word, clockwise or anti-clockwise.

28 Insert a word that means the same as the words outside the brackets.

BE EVASIVE (. . . . .) BUSHES

29 Make a six-letter word using only these four letters.

L O
G I

30 Grid

Each of the nine squares in the grid marked 1A to 3C should incorporate all the lines and symbols that are shown in the squares of the same letter and number immediately above and to the left. For example, 2B should incorporate all the lines and symbols that are in 2 and B.

One of the squares is incorrect. Which one is it?

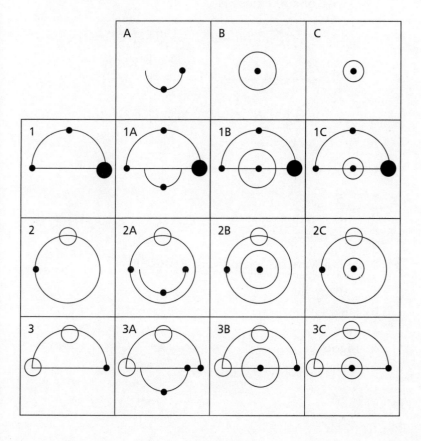

31 Which word means the same as NEGATORY?

   a) fallacious
   b) prodigious
   c) trifling
   d) restraining

32 Fill in the blanks to form two words which are synonyms, clockwise or anti-clockwise.

33 What is the value of x?

$$\frac{7}{9} \div \frac{5}{27} = x$$

34 What is always associated with FAIENCE?

   a) pottery
   b) fairies
   c) zinc
   d) ingots
   e) ghosts

35 Missing tile

Which of A–F is the missing tile?

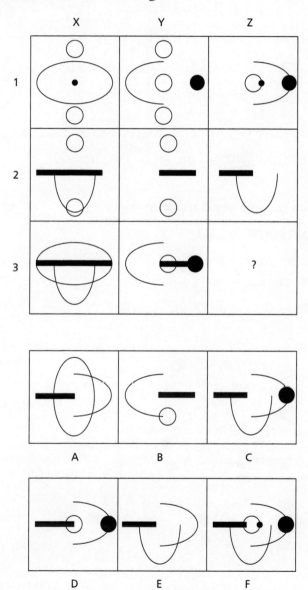

36 What is the value of x?

$4 \times 3 - 70 \div 10 + 6 = x$

37 What two words mean the opposite?

CONTRADICT, CALUMNY, DISINGENUOUS,
DETESTATION, INFAMOUS, CANDID

38 Place three two-letter bits together to make a PLANT.

CH – LL – CL – OR – BR – MA – ER – IC – OV

39 Solve the one-word anagram.

NINE PUGS

40 Odd one out

Which of these is the odd one out?

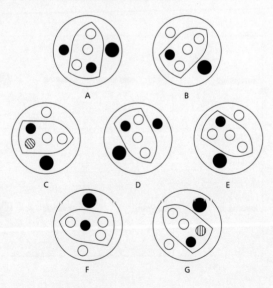

Test six

1 Pair a word in list A with its related adjective in list B.

List A	List B
FLUVIAL	ROOK
VERNAL	PARROT
PSITTACINE	RIVER
CORVID	SPRING

2 What number should replace the question mark?

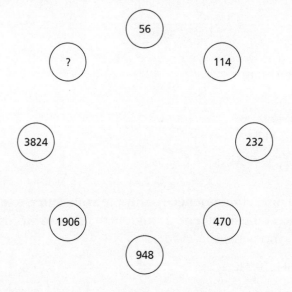

3 Comparison

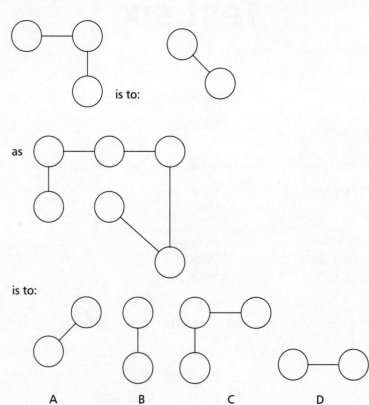

is to:

A   B   C   D

4 63 : 369
   47 : 7411
   86 : ?

5 Add one letter, not necessarily the same letter, to each word at the front, end or middle to find two words that are synonyms.

   RUSH, BEAK

6   Start at one of the corner squares and spiral clockwise round the perimeter to spell out a nine-letter word and finish at the centre square. You must provide the missing letters.

R	E	
A	R	
C	E	K

7   Which number comes next in the following sequence?

53472, 2435, 342, ?

8   Which of the following is not an anagram of an animal?

BRISK PONG
PUNCH KIM
RED OPAL
MOMS HOUR
FAB FOUL

9   What letter completes this sequence?

A B D O P Q ?

10   Which word in brackets means the same as the word in capitals?

PROGENY (skill, lineage, movement, progress, vocation)

11 Which three words can be inserted so that the phrase is palindromic, ie it reads the same backwards and forwards?

A DOG! . . . . A PAGODA

12 How many lines appear below?

13 Sequence

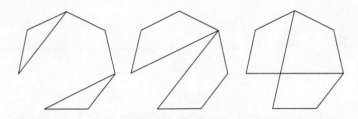

What comes next in the above sequence?

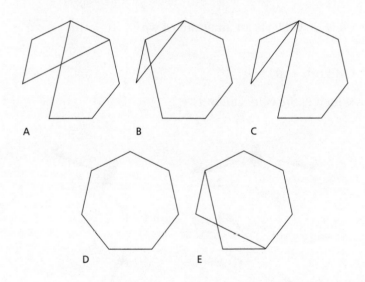

A   B   C

D   E

14 Below are eight CARING words. Take one letter from each
    of the eight words in turn to spell out a ninth CARING
    word.

    Clue: dependable

    FERVENT, CORDIAL, DOTING, DEVOTED, ATTACHED,
    FOND, AMOROUS, LOVING

15

You have a range of weights available from 1–10 units. They are all single weights. Which one should you use to balance the scale, and where should you place it?

16 OLD ELASTIC is an anagram of which 10-letter word?

17 Odd one out

Which is the odd one out?

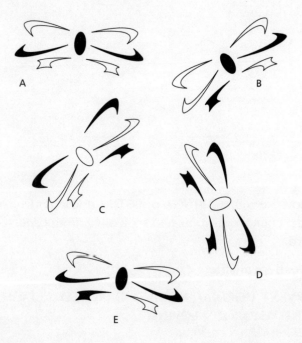

18 Find the phrase that has been hidden by removing the initial letter of each word, then removing the space between them.

    NHEEVEL

19 What number should replace the question mark?

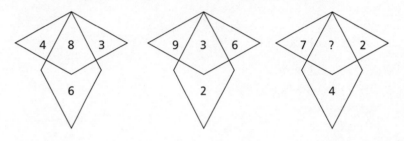

20 PERIGEE :   APOGEE
    PERIHELION : a) azimuth
                  b) eliptic
                  c) orrery
                  d) nadir
                  e) aphelion

21 Fill in the blanks, clockwise or anti-clockwise, to complete the word.

22 Which two words mean the same?

VERBOSE, MERCIFUL, CONCORDANT, MOMENTOUS,
MENIAL, PROLIX

23 Place three two-letter bits together to make a vegetable.

RA – EN – LE – RI – CI – DI – CE – VE – SH

24 What is a FERRULE?

a) a metal band
b) a circus wheel
c) a window
d) a funeral
e) rusty

25 Symbols

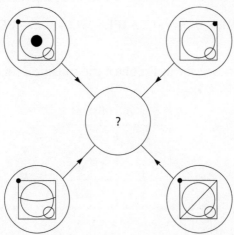

Each line and symbol that appears in the four outer circles, above, is transferred to the centre circle according to these rules:

if a line or symbol occurs in the outer circles:

once:	it is transferred
twice:	it is possibly transferred
3 times:	it is transferred
4 times:	it is not transferred.

Which of the circles A, B, C, D or E, shown below, should appear at the centre of the diagram, above?

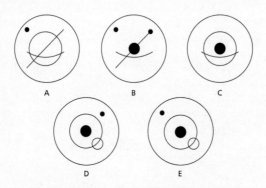

26 Place two three-letter bits together to make a dog.

TER – ZOE – BEA – SET – IER – GLI – BAS – BOR

27 What number should replace the question mark?

6	4	4	22
4	3	3	13
1	5	4	21
2	6	7	?

28 What number should replace the question mark?

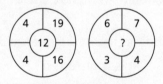

29 What is the name given to a group of KITTENS?

a) clutch
b) labour
c) swarm
d) kindle
e) sounder

30 Grid

Each of the nine squares in the grid marked 1A to 3C should incorporate all the lines and symbols that are shown in the squares of the same letter and number immediately above and to the left. For example, 2B should incorporate all the lines and symbols that are in 2 and B.

One of the squares is incorrect. Which one is it?

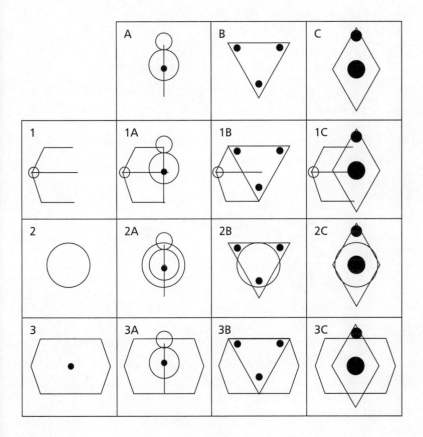

31 What is always associated with GENOA?

    a) a bustle
    b) haberdashery
    c) an eye glass
    d) a sail
    e) a short cloak

32 Solve the one-word anagram.

    IRON COPS

33 What number should replace the question mark?

    10, 1, 9, 6, 8, 11, 7, ?

34 Fill in the blanks, clockwise or anti-clockwise, to form two words that are synonyms.

35 Circles

Which of A, B, C, D or E fits into the blank circle to carry on a logical sequence?

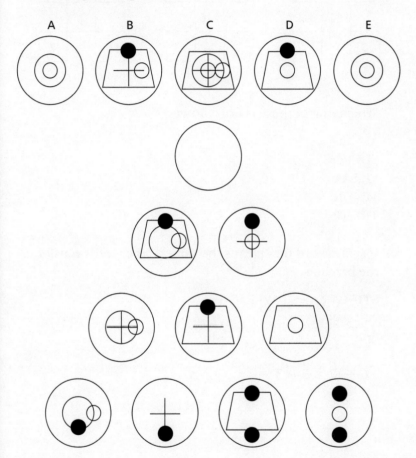

36 What number should replace the question mark?

4		12
	64	
8		4

3		9
	216	
3		12

20		9
	?	
6		2

37 Which one of these is not a flower?

ALEZAA
SUCROC
VILSAA
TEVOIL
TRYLUS

38 Insert a word that means the same as the words outside the brackets.

STINGY (. . . .) AVERAGE

39 Solve:

$-6 + (7 \times 8) - 3 \div 2 + 19 = x$

40 Comparison

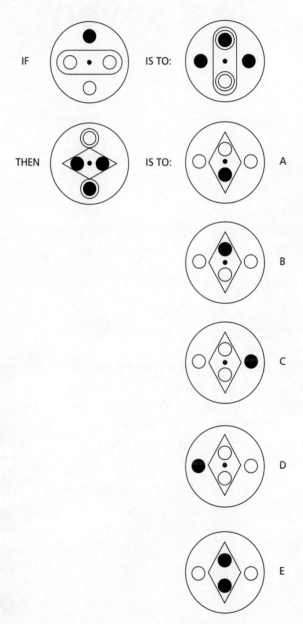

IF ... IS TO:

THEN ... IS TO: A

B

C

D

E

Test seven

1 Sequence

What comes next in the above sequence?

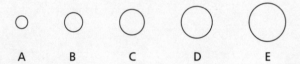

   A   B   C   D   E

2 Which other sport-related phrase can be placed in the right-hand column reading downwards in order to complete the six three-letter words reading across? The phrase you are looking for has two words (8, 4).

A	■	
C	U	
T	E	
I	■	
O	A	
N	■	
R	A	
E	■	
P	E	
L	■	
A	S	
Y	■	

3 Which word continues this sequence?

COUNTERFEIT, FLOUNDERING, ENCOUNTERED, SUBJOINDERS

Is it: viscountess, dumbfounded or preannounce?

4 What number should replace the question mark?

Clue: think laterally

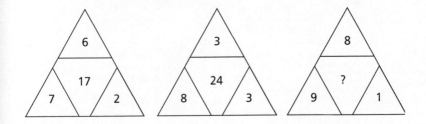

5 Which of the following is not an anagram of 'intelligence test'?

TESTING ELECT LINE
TESTING CLIENTELE
TIES GENTLE CLIENT
LET TESTING CLIENT
GET LITTLE INCENSE
ELICIT GENTLE NETS

6   Which of the numbers, from 1 to 121, appears in the grid twice, and which number is missing?

61	102	30	115	80	32	73	110	36	89	18
90	35	119	74	117	83	48	26	11	95	50
49	113	19	7	101	41	15	3	94	44	13
85	14	25	120	53	109	43	23	29	81	6
37	99	98	2	108	78	62	34	56	69	40
60	10	24	93	72	22	107	51	1	118	28
33	75	92	47	104	86	114	17	76	105	21
82	4	27	116	52	12	84	71	111	63	8
91	59	16	68	39	66	96	25	100	70	38
20	42	79	9	55	64	77	5	54	88	45
67	103	46	97	31	87	106	58	121	65	112

7   Which word in brackets is opposite in meaning to the word in capitals?

GRUESOME (enjoyable, appealing, wholesome, young, virtuous)

8   What number should replace the question mark?

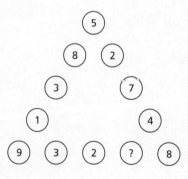

9 Solve the clues to find four six-letter words. The same three letters are represented by XYZ in each word.

X Y Z . . .   Clue: bovine animals
. X Y Z . .   Clue: attack with severe criticism
. . X Y Z .   Clue: find
. . . X Y Z   Clue: type of grape

10 Sequence

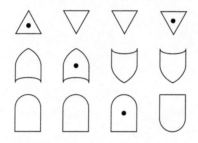

What comes next in the above sequence?

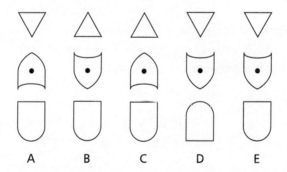

A   B   C   D   E

11 Change CAPRICORN to LIBRA. Each word repeats several letters from the word above it as indicated by *.

```
C A P R I C O R N
  * * * * * * .
. . * * * . .
    . . * * * .
      L I B R A
```

12 Find the starting point and follow the correct route from circle to circle to spell out a phrase (4, 2, 1, 3)

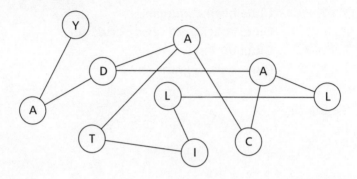

13 Insert a three-letter word that will complete the first word and start the second.

SEA (. . .) NET

14 A number of antonyms of the keyword are shown. Take one letter from each of the antonyms, in order, to spell out another antonym of the keyword.

KEYWORD : OMNIPOTENT

ANTONYMS : INFERIOR, IMPOTENT, POWERLESS, VULNERABLE, FRAIL, INCAPABLE

15 SUNDAY
MONDAY
WEDNESDAY
SATURDAY
WEDNESDAY

Which day comes next?

16 Sequence

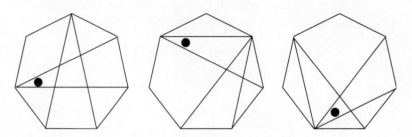

What comes next in the above sequence?

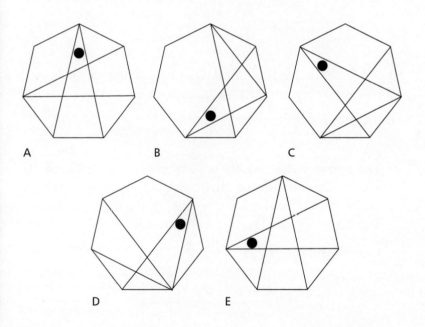

17 Visit each square once only and finish at the centre square to collect the treasure. 1E means one square East, 2W means two squares West.

1 E 1 S	1 S 1 W	2 W 2 S
2 E 1 S	**T**	1 S 1 W
1 E 2 N	2 N 1 E	2 W 2 N

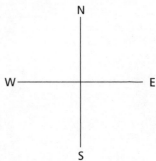

18 Solve each anagram to find two phrases that are spelt differently but sound alike, as in 'a name', 'an aim'.

WOKEN CANON   INTO NOON

19 The grid contains 25 different letters of the alphabet. What is the longest word that can be found by starting anywhere and working from square to square horizontally, vertically and diagonally, and not repeating a letter?

Clue: Significantly

Q	U	J	X	F
W	N	O	E	K
S	V	D	C	R
G	I	Y	A	H
P	M	L	B	T

20 What do the following have in common?

    TOTAL ECLIPSE
    A PIG IN A POKE
    WHITE ADMIRALS

21 Fill in the blanks, clockwise or anti-clockwise, to
    complete the word.

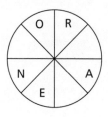

22 Which word means the same as ESOTERIC?

    a) pristine
    b) misshapen
    c) gibbous
    d) secret

23 What number should replace the question mark?

3		6		7		4		14		2
	42				80				?	
7		2		4		2		8		11

24 Solve the one-word anagram.

    IT CLAW'D

25 Circles

Which of A, B, C, D or E fits into the blank circle to carry on a logical sequence?

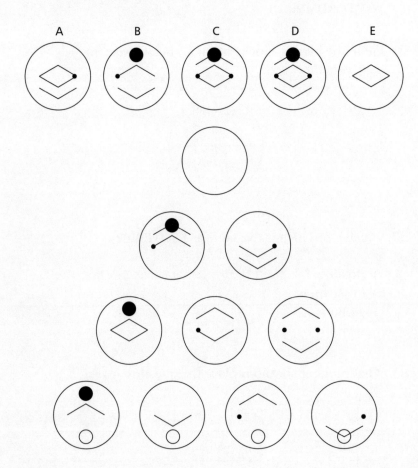

26 What number should replace the × ?

64	8	2	6
21	7	1	2
30	5	1	5
24	4	2	X

27 What is a GIGOT?

   a) a dancer
   b) a leg of mutton
   c) a rogue
   d) a measure
   e) a ravine

28 Place two three-letter bits together to make a FISH.

   KIP – ICY – PLA – MIN – PEN – NOW – HAD – DOK

29 Which two words mean the opposite?

   LICENTIOUS, CARP, FITFUL, CIRCUMSPECTION,
   APPROVE, DEMEANOUR

30 Symbols

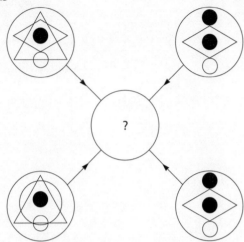

Each line and symbol that appears in the four outer circles, above, is transferred to the centre circle according to these rules:

if a line or symbol occurs in the outer circles:

once: it is transferred
twice: it is possibly transferred
3 times: it is transferred
4 times: it is not transferred.

Which of the circles A, B, C, D or E, shown below, should appear at the centre of the diagram, above?

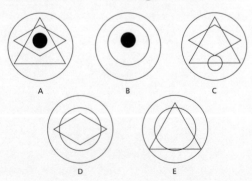

31 What is always associated with HASLET?

   a) food
   b) drink
   c) a machine
   d) a necklace
   e) a farm appliance

32 What number is to replace the question mark?

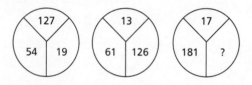

33 Fill in the blanks, clockwise or anti-clockwise, to form two
   words that are synonyms.

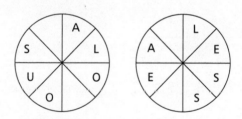

34 Make a six-letter word using only these four letters.

   LY
   GO

35 Grid

Each of the nine squares in the grid marked 1A to 3C should incorporate all the lines and symbols that are shown in the squares of the same letter and number immediately above and to the left. For example, 2B should incorporate all the lines and symbols that are in 2 and B.

One of the squares is incorrect. Which one is it?

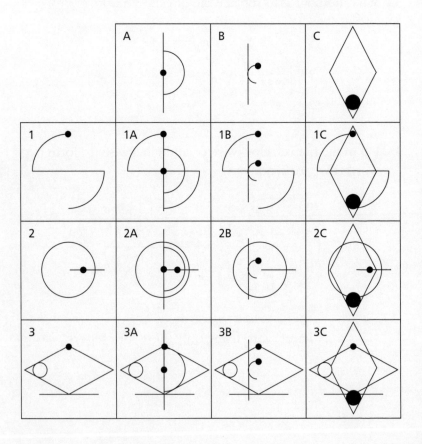

36 Insert a word that means the same as the words outside the brackets.

NOBLE (. . . .) KIND

37 What number should replace the question mark?

7, 14, 8, 10, 9, 6, 10, ?

38 What is the name given to a group of LARKS?

a) exaltation
b) badelynge
c) flock
d) pitying
e) run

39 Which one of these is not a musical instrument?

NILOIV
MATBAN
THIZRE
LAMYCB
DDIEFL

40 Hexagon

Which hexagon, A, B, C, D or E, fits the missing space?

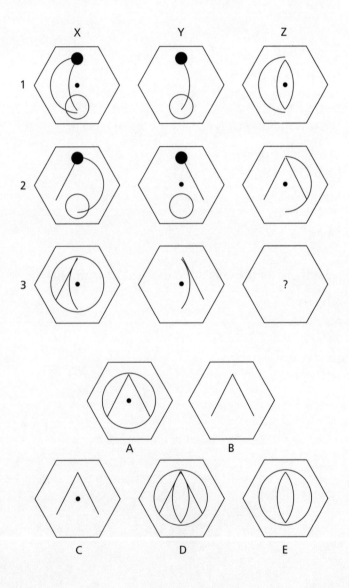

Test eight

1   Only one set of letters below can be arranged into a five-letter word. Can you find the word?

KIRCE
EMRUD
ONTDI
ENCID

2   What number should replace the question mark?

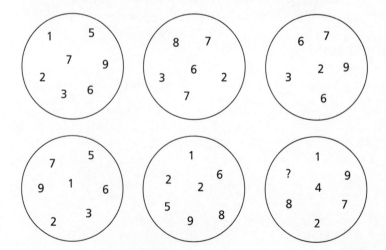

3   Solve the cryptic clue below. The answer is a 10-letter
    word anagram contained within the clue.

> INCLEMENT
> WEATHER
> SPOILT
> MINOR ARTS

4   What famous building can be inserted into the bottom line
    to complete nine three-letter words reading downwards?

T	O	W	E	R	O	F	L	O	N	D	O	N
	B	A	A		W	E	A			I	D	I

5   In a game of 10 players lasting for 30 minutes, five
    reserves substitute each player, so that all players,
    including reserves, are on the pitch for the same
    length of time. How long is each player on the pitch?

6   Comparison

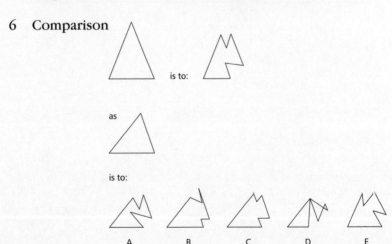

is to:

as

is to:

A   B   C   D   E

7

25	13	10	1	17
8	24	11	12	4
19	6	21	7	5
9	15	5	18	3
14	20	22	16	2

What number is two places away from itself, plus 3, three places away from itself doubled, two places away from itself minus 2, two places away from itself plus 4, two places away from itself minus 1, and two places away from itself plus 6?

8 Start at one of the corner squares and spiral clockwise round the perimeter to spell out a nine-letter word, finishing at the centre square. You must provide the missing letters.

F	E	A
E	T	T
		I

9 Comparison

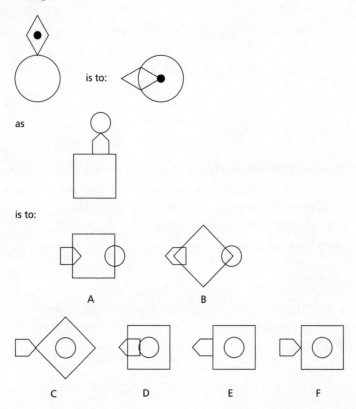

10

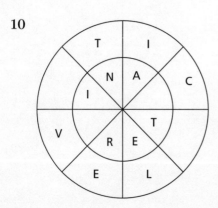

Complete two words, one reading clockwise round the inner circle and one round the outer circle. You must provide the missing letters. The two words are related in that they form a phrase.

11 Add one letter, not necessarily the same letter, to each word at the front, end or middle to find two words that are synonyms.

COOK, HEAT

12 Which word in brackets is opposite in meaning to the word in capitals?

SURREPTITIOUS (servile, trusty, scarce, overt, unauthorized)

13 What number continues this sequence?

1, 4, 8, 13, 19, ?

14 Solve the two anagrams below to create a familiar phrase.

Clue: Low-cost curiosity

. P .... F ..   ... R T ....
↑ FRY ONE PAN ↑   ↑ YOU HURT GHOST ↑

15 Which is the odd one out?

MOGUL, SHANG, TANG, MING, HAN

16 GENEALOGY : ANCESTRY
ETYMOLOGY : a) knowledge
             b) insects
             c) fossils
             d) inscriptions
             e) words

17 What number should replace the question mark?

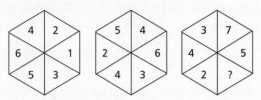

18 What three letters can be inserted into the brackets to spell out a girl's name when added to the first three letters and placed in front of the second three letters?

MAR (. . .) RON

19 Sequence

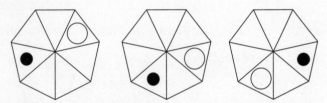

Which option below continues the above sequence?

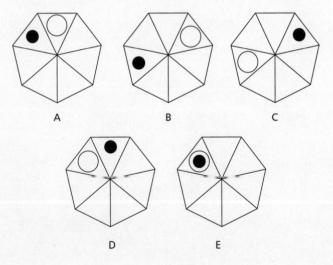

20 Odd one out

Which of these clock faces is the odd one out?

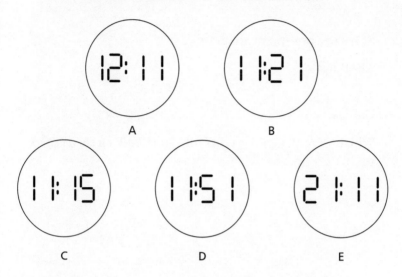

21 What number should replace the question mark?

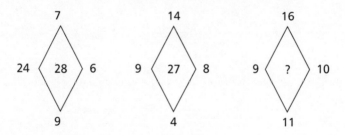

22 What have the five words in common?

KNELL
STAPLE
SNORED
REMOTE
SUGGEST

23 What number should replace the question mark?

   1   11   21   1211   111221   ?

24 Solve the one-word anagram.

   TRAILING

25 Circles

   Which of A, B, C, D or E fits into the blank circle to carry
   on the sequence?

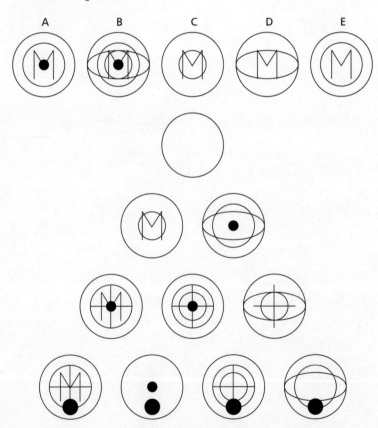

26 Fill in the blanks, clockwise or anti-clockwise, to complete the word.

27 Place two three-letter bits together to make an insect.

SPI, LOC, ADA, IST, SPI, CIC, DAR, DIR

28 What number should replace the question mark?

29 What is STOCCADO?

   a) a stockade
   b) fast talking
   c) a dance
   d) a fencing stroke
   e) illness

30 Symbols

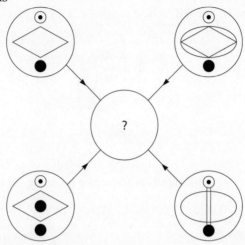

Each line and symbol that appears in the four outer circles, above, is transferred to the centre circle according to these rules:

if a line or symbol occurs in the outer circles:

once:	it is transferred
twice:	it is possibly transferred
3 times:	it is transferred
4 times:	it is not transferred.

Which of the circles A, B, C, D or E, shown below, should appear at the centre of the diagram, above?

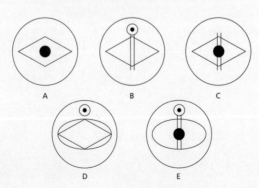

31 Which two words mean the same?

OBVIATE, LACERATE, INTIMIDATE, ENDANGER,
REPUDIATE, DISCLAIM

32 Insert a word that means the same as the words outside
the brackets.

EQUAL (. . . .) LOOK CLOSELY

33 What is the name given to a group of PEACOCKS?

a) bevy
b) ostentation
c) lepe
d) richesse
e) rayful

34 What number should replace the question mark?

12, 1, 10, 4, 8, 7, 6, ?

35 Hexagon

Which hexagon, A, B, C, D or E, fits the missing space?

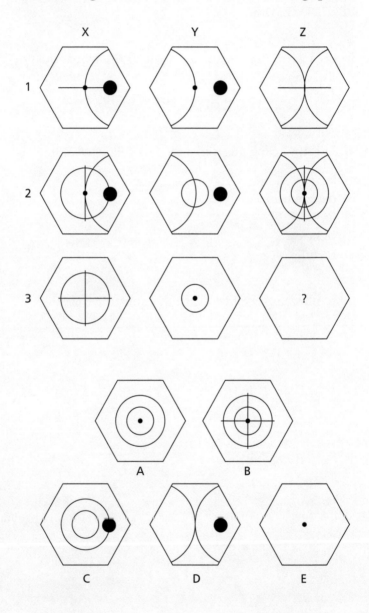

36 What is always associated with INCARNADINE?

   a) imprisonment
   b) body language
   c) teeth
   d) flesh coloured
   e) quarries

37 What number should replace the question mark?

38 Fill in the blanks, clockwise or anti-clockwise, to form two words that are synonyms.

39 Which one of these is not a weather term?

   YLILHC
   YTOSMR
   SUMPOS
   WEROHS
   ULQLSA

40 Boxes

Which of the five boxes below has the most in common
with the box on the right?

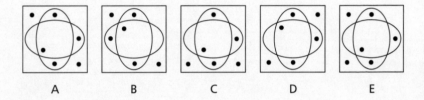

A   B   C   D   E

Test nine

1

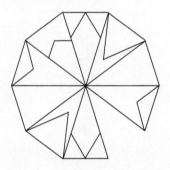

Find the missing section from the options below.

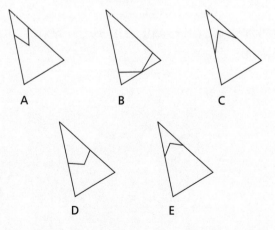

A   B   C

D   E

2 Read clockwise to spell two antonyms by selecting one letter from each circle. Every letter is used and each word starts in a different circle.

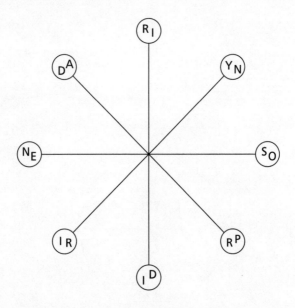

3 Which word in brackets means the same as the word in capitals?

METAPHYSICAL (transient, esoteric, symbolic, planned, fastidious)

4 Comparison

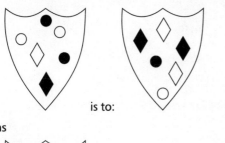

is to:

as

is to:

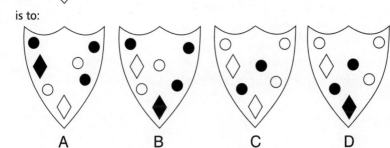

A   B   C   D

5 What number should replace the question mark?

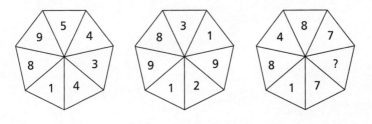

6   Solve each anagram to find two phrases that are spelt
     differently but sound alike, as in 'a name', 'an aim'.

     IMPEL UP   MY EEL PUP

7   What do these words have in common?

     PREFERABLE, PURVEYED, TARADIDDLE, BAGPIPES,
     BEJEWELLED

8   The words BEST and WORST are opposite in meaning.
     Find two more words that are opposite in meaning, one
     that must rhyme with BEST and one that must rhyme
     with WORST.

9   Odd one out

     Four of these pieces can be fitted together to form a
     perfect square. Which is the odd one out?

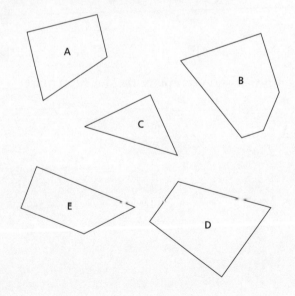

10 Missing tile

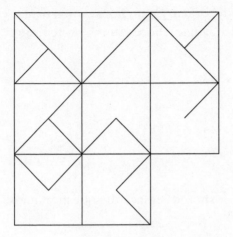

Choose the missing tile from the options below.

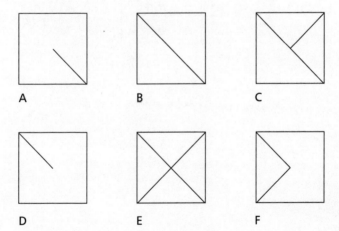

11 Which is the odd one out?

Broth, elate, organ, glean, horse, idler, dance, eager, throb, groan, riled, angle, shore, caned, owned, agree, endow

12 SPIN   = 52
   LIST   = 51
   CALM = 91
   LOAD = 62
   LAND = ?

13 What letter should replace the question mark?

?	E	D	D
A	S	L	E
N	A	A	R
S	N	D	S

14 Odd one out

Which is the odd one out?

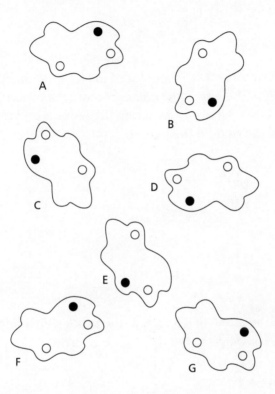

15 Read clockwise to find two eight-letter words that are antonyms. You have to find the starting point and provide the missing letters.

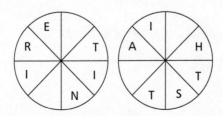

16 The phrase train-spotting (5–8) is an anagram of which other familiar phrase (8–5)?

Clue: take the first step

17 A B C D E F G H

What letter is two to the right of the letter immediately to the left of the letter that comes mid-way between the letter immediately to the left of the letter H and the letter two to the right of the letter A?

18 7461 :   135

6893 : a) 151
　　　 b) 179
　　　 c) 152
　　　 d) 161
　　　 e) 125

19 Insert the name of a fruit into the brackets reading downwards to complete the three-letter words.

BI (.)
LE (.)
HA (.)
HI (.)
TO (.)
FA (.)

20 What number should replace the question mark?

	1				4				1	
9	2	6		7	8	8		3	?	6

21 Which word means the same as ESPALIER?

    a) wooden trellis
    b) spectre
    c) advocate
    d) ligament

22 What number should replace the question mark?

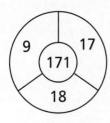 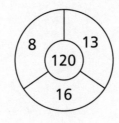 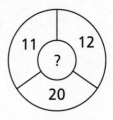

23 Solve the one-word anagram.

THE ACHE

24 What number should replace the question mark?

22, 21, 30, ?, 38, 37, 46

25 Comparison

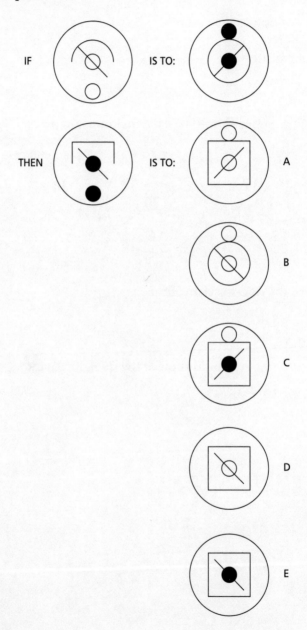

IF ... IS TO:

THEN ... IS TO: A

B

C

D

E

26 Fill in the blanks, clockwise or anti-clockwise, to complete the word.

27 Which two words mean the opposite?

CORPOREAL, IMPUDENT, SPIRITUAL, ABUNDANCE, FAULTLESS, CONFORMITY

28 What is a WASSERMAN?

    a) a guard
    b) a bird
    c) a slave
    d) a fish
    e) a sea monster

29 What is the value of x ?

$$\frac{3}{5} \div \frac{39}{125} = x$$

30 Circles

Which of A, B, C, D or E fits into the blank circle to carry on a logical sequence?

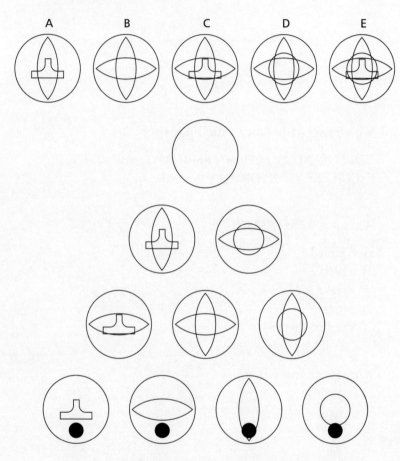

31 Make a six-letter word using only these four letters.

LO
TE

32 What number should replace the question mark?

6, 11, 8½, 7, 11, 3, 13½, ?

33 What is the name given to a group of WOODCOCK?

a) dray
b) hover
c) fall
d) nide
e) parliament

34 Insert a word that means the same as the words outside
the brackets.

PESTER (. . . . . .) TYPE OF ANIMAL

35 Symbols

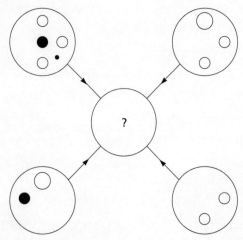

Each line and symbol that appears in the four outer circles, above, is transferred to the centre circle according to these rules:

if a line or symbol occurs in the outer circles:

once: it is transferred
twice: it is possibly transferred
3 times: it is transferred
4 times: it is not transferred.

Which of the circles A, B, C, D or E, shown below, should appear at the centre of the diagram, above?

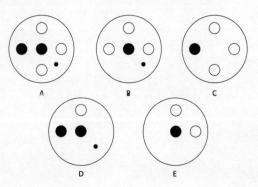

36 Fill in the blanks, clockwise or anti-clockwise, to form two
    words that are synonyms.

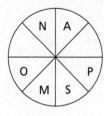   

37 What is the symbol for $\sqrt{-1}$?

38 What is always associated with LUFF?

    a) heartiness
    b) sincerity
    c) misery
    d) clouds
    e) wind

39 What number should replace the question mark?

    1, 24, 816, 3264, 12825, 651210, ?

40 Odd one out

Which of these is the odd one out?

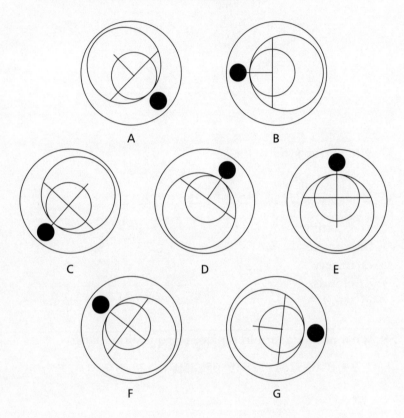

Test ten

1   Which number is the odd one out?

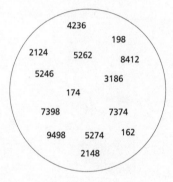

2   Spiral clockwise to find a 10-letter word. Only alternate letters are shown.

Clue: outwit

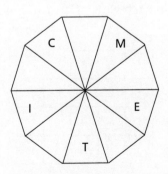

3 Comparison

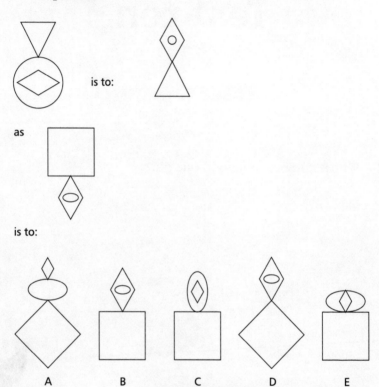

A   B   C   D   E

4 Each square contains the letters of a nine-letter word. The two words are synonyms, and the overlapping letters T and A appear in each word. Can you unscramble them?

D	E	R		
E	C	T	M	E
I	A	A	L	I
	N	E	I	

5   Find the starting point and track from letter to letter
     along the lines to spell out an item of jewellery (8, 4).

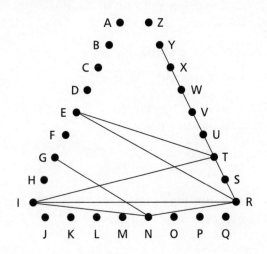

6   Squares

Which of the squares below has most in common with the
square above?

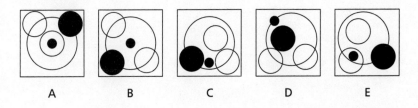

7 If presented with the words MAR, AM and FAR and asked to find the shortest word that contained all the letters from which these words could be produced, you should come up with the word FARM.

Here is a further list of words:

ANGRY, LYNCH, MAGIC

What is the shortest English word from which all these words can be produced?

Clue: captivatingly

8 Which box of numbers (A, B, C or D) should replace the box of question marks?

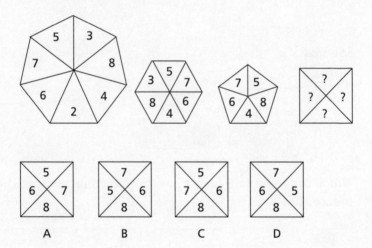

9 Boxes

To which of the boxes below can a dot be added so that it meets the same conditions as in the box above?

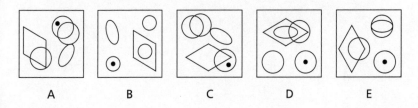

A   B   C   D   E

10 What number should replace the question mark?

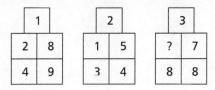

11 Read clockwise to find two words, one in each circle, that are antonyms. You must provide the missing letters.

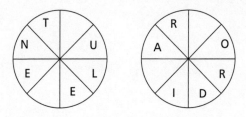

12 What number comes next in this sequence?

100, 99, 117, 108, ?

13 Comparison

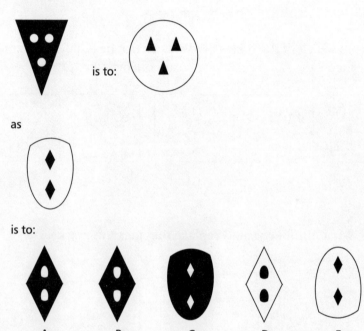

14 Read along the connecting lines from circle to circle to spell out a well-known phrase, especially at a certain time of the year (6, 4).

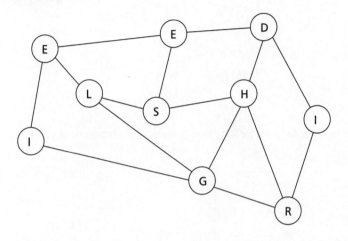

15 What word is both a weaving machine and means 'to menace'?

16 CRUSH VIOLA is an anagram of which 10-letter word?

17 Sequence

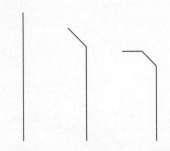

Which option below continues the above sequence?

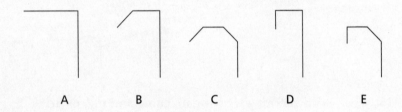

A   B   C   D   E

18 What number comes next in this sequence?

1, 1.5, 2.5, 4, ?

19 Only one set of letters below can be arranged into a five-letter word. Can you find the word?

MUCHO
WINFO
ALPIC
DEPNU
BRENU

20 What word replaces the question marks in order to form seven five-letter words sandwiched between the letters on the right and the left?

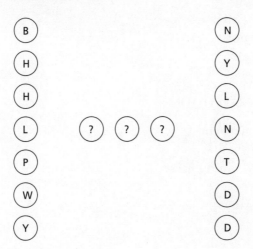

21 Fill in the blanks, clockwise and anti-clockwise, to complete the word.

22 What is always associated with NUX VOMICA?

   a) gunpowder
   b) an organ
   c) strychnine
   d) smelling salts
   e) hymns

23 Which is the odd one out?

   a) ballista
   b) ventage
   c) arquebus
   d) claymore
   e) bazooka

24 What is ZAPATEADO?

   a) a moustache
   b) a dance
   c) a drumming noise
   d) a dish
   e) a flower

25 Odd one out

Which is the odd one out?

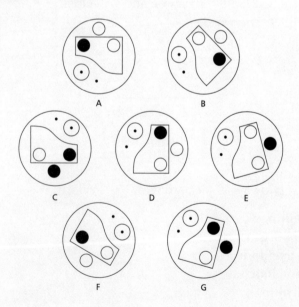

26 What is the meaning of NUBILE?

   a) lithe
   b) charismatic
   c) marriageable
   d) thoughtful
   e) myopic

27 Insert a word that means the same as the words outside
   the brackets.

   DOG (. . . . .) SPORTSMAN

28 What is the name given to a group of DUCKS?

   a) paddling
   b) fesnyng
   c) knob
   d) muster
   e) plump

29 Place two three-letter bits together to make a FRUIT.

   ORA – PAP – PIN – PAW – PAR – PIP – AYE – NGI

30 Circles

Which of A, B, C, D or E fits into the blank circle to carry on the sequence?

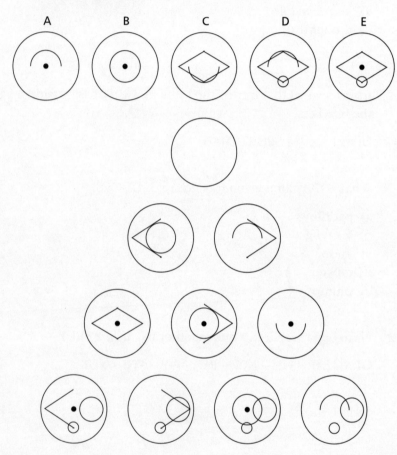

31 What number should replace the question mark?

1, 4, 13, 40, 121, ?

32 Which two words mean the same?

INDUSTRIOUS, BEARING, BUSINESS, MIEN, PANACEA, IMPIETY

33 Solve the one-word anagram.

SOBBING

34 What number should replace the question mark?

35 Symbols

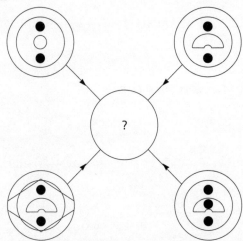

Each line and symbol that appears in the four outer circles, above, is transferred to the centre circle according to these rules:

if a line or symbol occurs in the outer circles:

once:	it is transferred
twice:	it is possibly transferred
3 times:	it is transferred
4 times:	it is not transferred.

Which of the circles A, B, C, D or E, shown below, should appear at the centre of the diagram, above?

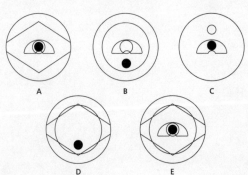

36 Which number should replace the question mark?

4, 12, 7½, 10½, 11, 9, 14½, ?

37 Fill in the blanks, clockwise or anti-clockwise, to form two words that are synonyms.

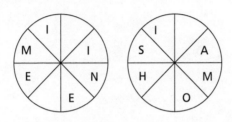

38 Find a word to replace the dots that means the same as the words outside the brackets.

WEIGHT (. . . . .) LYNX

39 Find a word to replace the dots to make five new words.

DISCORD
GALL
SEC
ERR
PAGE

(. . .)

40 Circles

Which of A, B, C, D or E fits into the blank circle to carry on a logical sequence?

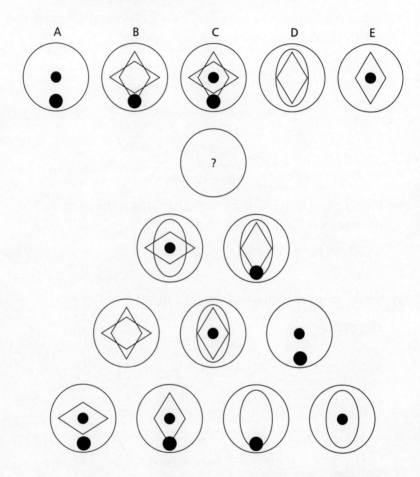

Test one

Answers

1 Vast melody

2 Fjord; it is a stretch of water. The others are all land.

3 6; $4 \times 9 = 36$

4 Reef; to spell out the numbers as follows:
   CART(ONE)NJOYMEN(TWO)RDSMI(THREE)F

5 E; a dot is only carried forward when it appears in the same position in two of the previous three circles.

6 Talent

7 27; add, then deduct, the sum of the digits of the previous number alternately each time, ie $36 - 3 - 6 = 27$

8 Delete; to give: fade/desk, hole/lean, kite/tear

9 48 mph
   Say, distance travelled = 60 miles each way

   therefore journey out = $\dfrac{60}{40}$ = 1.5 hours

   journey in = $\dfrac{60}{60}$ = 1 hour

   120 mile journey = $\dfrac{120}{2.5}$ = 48 mph

10 Abundance

11 c) across

12 Double-page spread

13 A; the figure rotates into an upright position anti-clockwise. Black turns white and white turns black.

14

4	14	•15	1
9	•7	6	12
5	11	10	•8
•16	2	3	13

15 They all contain trees: le(gum)es, qu(ash)ed, af(fir)ms, cl(oak)ed

16 $51; 9 \times 5 = 45 + 6 = 51$

17 When prosperity comes, do not use all of it.

18 Long, pithy

19 0; looking down and across the sum of alternate numbers are equal, for example
$7 + 9 = 10 + 6$

20 Never look a gift horse in the mouth.

21 a) recluse

22 $64 - (12 \times 2) + (6 \div 3) = 42$
The rule is $\times$, $\div$, $+$, $-$ taken in that order.

23 Butchery, massacre

24 Clear soup

25 1A

26 Polecat

27 Grill

28 31; increase by 5 in a clockwise fashion every three sectors
ie 1, 6, 11, 16, 21, 26, 31, 36.

29 Feeler

30 E; the two lower circles join together to form the circle
above, but similar symbols disappear.

31 Disparage, praise

32 c) building

33 Dam

34 $\dfrac{5}{6} \div \dfrac{1}{7} = \dfrac{5}{6} \times \dfrac{7}{1} = \dfrac{35}{6} = 5\dfrac{5}{6}$

35 A; x + y = z
       1 + 2 = 3
   But similar symbols disappear.

36 Escudo

37 e) a compass

38 Frigidly

39 67; (7 × 8) − 8 = 48
       (9 × 7) − 5 = 58
       (11 × 5) − 7 = 48
       (6 × 12) − 5 = 67

40 A

Test two

Answers

1 14

2 Vulnerable

3 Wednesday

4 In the pink

5 Antipodean

6 Rise to vote sir

7 B

8 7, 21, 22

9 Sack oboe = bookcase. The books are lexicon (Neil Cox), thesaurus (assure hut), omnibus (sumo bin) and cookery (Roy Coke).

10 Modest

11 Fox

12 14; $14^2 = 196$

13 Halt, start

14 B; A is the same as E rotated, and C is the same as D.

15 Fresh – water – fall – short – story – line – age – group

16 28, 102; $7 \times 4 = 28, 74 + 28 = 102$

17 Pen; it is a female swan. The rest are all male animals.

18 Picture-gallery

19 24; $24336 \times 2 = 48672$, ie the number formed at the top half of the decagon is double the number formed by the bottom half.

20 Exultation

21 Ringworm

22 d) basketwork

23 Fob

24 Crocodile

25 B; A same as D
    F same as G
    E same as C

26 55;   61   54   62   55   63   56   64
            −7   +8   −7   +8   −7   +8

27 e) an onlooker

28 Acacia

29 Rock

30 D; the two lower circles combine to form the circle
    above, unlike symbols disappear.

31 Lambent, flickering

32 Derision, contempt

33 d) novice

34 $\dfrac{4}{13} \div \dfrac{9}{52} = \dfrac{4}{13} \times \dfrac{52}{9} = \dfrac{16}{9} = 1\dfrac{7}{9}$

35 B; x + y = z
 1 + 2 = 3
But similar symbols disappear.

36 45; (7 + 6) × 4 = 52
 (9 + 3) × 5 = 60
 (10 + 5) × 4 = 60
 (8 + 7) × 3 = 45

37 (7 × 9) – (3 × 4) + 10 = 61
The rule is ×, ÷, +, – taken in that order.

38 e) glean

39 30; 9 – 6 = 3   7 – 3 = 4   8 – 2 = 6
 7 + 7 = 14   6 + 4 = 10   3 + 2 = 5

40 2A

Test three

Answers

1 Paragraph; the vowel is O.

2 Jacksonville

3 D; each time two symbols touch they disappear at the next stage and are replaced by two new symbols.

4

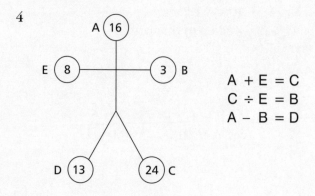

A + E = C
C ÷ E = B
A − B = D

5 Auld Lang Syne

6 I scream, ice cream

7 18; 14 × 4 = 56,   4 × 4 = 16,   8 × 4 = 32
9 × 4 = 36,   7 × 4 = 28,   5 × 4 = 20

8 One man band; to give: ago, fan, hue, dim, lea, pan, hob, pea, man, wad.

9 Embroidery (my dire robe)

10 b) flag

11 E; all the others are made up of three identical shapes.

12 Supplication, plea

13 –2; 1 (+1) = 2, 2 (–2) =   0,
          0 (+3) = 3, 3 (–4) = –1,
          –1 (+5) = 4, 4 (–6) = –2

14 The Old Man and the Sea (Ernest Hemingway); to give:
    hothead, scolded, romance, slander, dithery, roseate

15 4; the numbers represent the numbers of consonants in
    each word of the question.

16 E; the black circle moves one left, three right;
        the line moves one right, three left;
        the tower moves two left, one right;
        the white circle moves one right, two left.

17 RUE; each letter moves forward three places in the alphabet:

    O P Q **R**
    R S T **U**
    B C D **E**

18 45; 13 × 4 = 52 – 7 = 45

19 Lax/lacks

20 Avoid

21 Horrific

22 176;   6 + 7 = 13   11 + 12 = 23   17 + 5 = 22
         10 − 2 = $\underline{8}$ ×   6 − 3 = $\underline{3}$ ×   10 − 2 = $\underline{8}$ ×
                   104   69   176

23 c) stone

24 Pan

25 C

26 a) a charm

27 $\dfrac{5}{11} \div \dfrac{15}{44} = \dfrac{5}{11} \times \dfrac{44}{15} = \dfrac{4}{3} = 1\dfrac{1}{3}$

28 Magpie

29 Fizgig

30 E

31 Hail

32 −8 + (6 × 8) − (2 × 5) = 30
   The rule is ×, ÷, +, − taken in that order.

33 Handsome, pleasing

34 a) a mathematical term

35 2B

36 Gratuitous, free

37 Alligators

38 32; $4 \div 2 \times 8 = 16$
$\ 6 \div 3 \times 7 = 14$
$\ 9 \div 3 \times 8 = 24$
$\ 8 \div 4 \times 16 = 32$

39 28;   27   31   28   32   29   33   30
 +4   −3   +4   −3   +4   −3

40 D; $x + y = z$
$\ 1 + 2 = 3$
But similar symbols disappear.

Test four

Answers

1 Clarion; all the others have a keyboard.

2 At a loss for words

3 46284; take the even numbers in reverse order.

4 None of them repeat a letter.

5 D; there are three different top symbols and three
   different bottom (inverted) symbols in each horizontal
   line and vertical column of shields.

6 Molecule, particle

7 c) mansard : roof

8 Folly

9 9, 11; start at the top right-hand square and spiral to the
   centre following the route shown in the sequence −2, +1,
   +2

7	5	4	6	— START
5	8	10	8	
6	9	11	7	
8	6	7	9	

10 They can all be prefixed with semi, ie semiprecious,
   semicircle, semitone, semi-automatic.

11 Keep the ball rolling.

12 8; the top three lines added together equal the bottom
   line: 27684 + 12196 + 25478 = 65358

13 13211A; each group describes the one before, ie one 3, two 1s, one A.

14

D	A	M	P			
A	R	E	A			
M	E	W	S			
P	A	S	T	I	M	E
			I	D	O	L
			M	O	S	S
			E	L	S	E

15 C; one is a mirror image of the other.

16 Evacuation; it repeats the letter a. All the other words have the vowels a, e, i, o, u, once only.

17 7984; in all the others multiply the middle two digits to obtain the first and fourth digits, for example 5964, where 9 × 6 = 54.

18 Knavish, principled

19 Thunder storm, to give: hat, hen, pad, rue, ear, sit, elm.

20 Martin, which is an anagram of Antrim.
Strode is an anagram of Dorset; milk, rice an anagram of Limerick; and Edna, beer an anagram of Aberdeen.

21 Hide

22 Out

23 9; opposite segments add to 12.

24 b) Haras

25 A

26 Urbanity, breeding

27 a)   A clockwork model

28 $\dfrac{17}{19} \div \dfrac{3}{38} = \dfrac{17}{\cancel{19}} \times \dfrac{\cancel{38}^{2}}{3} = \dfrac{34}{3} = 11\dfrac{1}{3}$

29 Dihras = radish

30 B; x + y = z
       1 + 2 = 3
But similar symbols disappear.

31 132; $\begin{matrix}16 - 4 = 12 \\ 3 + 3 = 6\end{matrix}\times$ $\begin{matrix}17 - 1 = 16 \\ 8 + 2 = 10\end{matrix}\times$ $\begin{matrix}14 - 3 = 11 \\ 8 + 4 = 12\end{matrix}\times$

32 Astronomers

33 Lampoon, defame

34 Wind

35 E

36 c) a messenger

37 Pinwheel

38 $3 - (6 \times 7) + (6 \div 4) = -37\frac{1}{2}$
The rule is $\times$, $\div$, $+$, $-$ taken in that order

39 Donkey

40 3A

Test five

Answers

1   14

2   Enable, length, thieve, vendor, oracle, lessen.

3   1.5 minutes

$$\frac{1}{3} + \frac{1}{2} - \frac{1}{6} = 0.33 + 0.5 - 0.166 = 0.66$$

$$\frac{1}{0.66} = 1.5 \text{ minutes}$$

4 B; the large arc moves 45° anti-clockwise. The two remaining arcs move 90° anti-clockwise.

5 Tap; all the other three-letter words are spelt out by alternate letters of one of the seven-letter words, for example AST*O*UN*D* = SON

6 53; 3 + 2 = 5   2 + 1 = 3

7 They all contain Biblical characters:
ABUN(DAN)CE, AL(LEVI)ATE, UNT(RUTH)S,
PRO(CAIN)E, C(HAM)BER

8 P; there are 15 letters before it in the alphabet, and ten after.

9 Flush toilet

10 C; it repeats the second flag with left and right reversed in the same way that the third flag repeats the first flag.

11

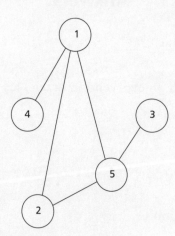

12 Fragrant, aromatic

13 Simpler tax

14 d) invent

15 Meet – encounter (truce none)

16 698; the numbers 98725136 are being repeated in the same order.

17 Professional

18 27; there are two sequences running alternately. The first starts with 7 and goes +2, +3, +4 etc. The second starts with 8 and goes +2, +4, +6 etc.

19 Vagrant, itinerant

20 Put on ice

21 XESTTE = SEXTET

22 55; $8 \div 2 = 4$ $9 \div 3 = 3$ $10 \div 2 = 5$

$11 + 7 = \dfrac{18}{72} \times$ $12 + 6 = \dfrac{18}{54} \times$ $2 + 9 = \dfrac{11}{55} \times$

23 Picture

24 c) draught

25 C; the two lower circles combine to form the circle above but similar symbols disappear.

26 a) a vehicle

27 Insomuch

28 Hedge

29 Gigolo

30 1A

31 c) trifling

32 Innocent, virtuous

33 $\dfrac{7}{9} \div \dfrac{5}{27} = \dfrac{7}{9} \times \dfrac{27}{5} = \dfrac{21}{5} = 4\dfrac{1}{5}$

34 a) pottery

35 F; $x + y = z$
$\quad\;\; 1 + 2 = 3$
But similar symbols disappear.

36 $(4 \times 3) - (70 \div 10) + 6 = 11$
The rule is $\times$, $\div$, $+$, $-$ taken in that order.

37 Disingenuous, candid

38 Clover

39 Penguins

40 F; A is the same as D
       B is the same as E
       C is the same as G

Test six

Answers

1 Fluvial/river, psittacine/parrot, corvid/rook, vernal/spring.

2 7662; start at 56 and work clockwise as follows:
   + 1 × 2, + 2 × 2, + 3 × 2, + 4 × 2 etc.
   For example (56 + 1) × 2 = 114, (114 + 2) × 2 = 232

3 D; only circles connected to one other circle are carried
   forward and a line is then drawn between them.

4 6814; reverse the digits and add together to obtain the
   final digits.

5 Crush, break

6 Caretaker

7 23; discard the highest digit each time, then reverse the
   remaining digits.

8 MOMS HOUR = MUSHROOM. The animals are: springbok
(brisk pong), chipmunk (punch Kim), leopard (red opal)
and buffalo (fab foul)

9 R; only letters with an enclosed area as printed.

10 Lineage

11 A dog! A panic in a pagoda.

12 11

13 E; the two lines are moving one corner at a time at each
stage, one clockwise, the other anti-clockwise.

14 Faithful

15

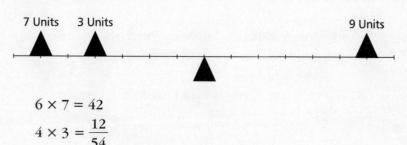

$$6 \times 7 = 42$$
$$4 \times 3 = \frac{12}{54}$$
$$= \quad 9 \times 6 \ (54)$$

16 Oscillated

17 B; A is the same as D with black/white reversal;
C is the same as E with black/white reversal.

18 On the level

19 14; 7 × 4 = 28 ÷ 2 = 14

20 e) aphelion

21 GALLIPOT

22 Verbose, prolix

23 Endive

24 a) a metal band

25 B

26 Basset

27 44; 6 + (4 × 4) = 22
   4 + (3 × 3) = 13
   1 + (5 × 4) = 21
   2 + (6 × 7) = 44

28 30; 4 × 19 = 76   6 × 7 = 42
   $4 \times 16 = \dfrac{64}{12}$ – $3 \times 4 = \dfrac{12}{30}$ –

29 d) kindle

30 3B

31 d) a sail

32 Scorpion

33 16; There are two series:

-1   10, 9, 8, 7

+5   1, 6, 11, 16

34 Dreadful, shocking

35 C; the lower two circles combine to produce the circle above but like symbols disappear.

36 120; $4 \times 4 = 16$ $3 \times 12 = 36$ $20 \times 2 = 40$

$12 - 8 = \dfrac{4}{64} \times$ $9 - 3 = \dfrac{6}{216} \times$ $9 - 6 = \dfrac{3}{120} \times$

37 Trylus = sultry

38 Mean

39 $-6 + 56 - 1\frac{1}{2} + 19 = 67\frac{1}{2}$

40 A

Test seven

Answers

1 A; there are two alternate sequences. In the first the circles are getting smaller, in the second they are getting larger.

2 Starting post; to give: cut, tea, oat, ran, pep, ass

3 Dumbfounded; in each word the letters ONE are moving up one place, ie
. O . N . E . . . . ., . . O . N . E . . . . etc.

4 6; the number in the first triangle is arrived at by adding the numbers at the top, ie 6 + 3 + 8 = 17. Similarly, 7 + 8 + 9 = 24, and 2 + 3 + 1 = 6

5 Let testing client

6 25 appears twice, 57 is missing

7 Appealing

8 4; the total of numbers on each side is 26.

9 XYZ = CAT; cattle, scathe, locate, muscat

10 B; at each stage the dot moves down one. After it has appeared in a figure, that figure becomes inverted.

11 C A P R I C O R N
   A P R I C O T
D E P R I V E
   S L I V E R
    L I B R A
Variations are possible.

12 Call it a day

13 Season, sonnet

14 Feeble

15 Monday; skip an extra day at each stage.

16 E; each triangle stays on its same base but its apex moves.
The triangle with the dot moves one clockwise, two anti-
clockwise etc. The other triangle moves in exactly the
same way.

17 Move as follows:

8	5	3
6	T	1
4	2	7

18 Known ocean, no notion

19 Considerably

20 All contain a drink:

TOT(AL E)CLIPSE
A PI(G IN) A POKE
WHI(TE A)DMIRALS

21 Forsaken

22 d) secret

23 48; $7 \times 6 = 42$ $\times 42$ $4 \times 4 = 16$ $\times 80$ $8 \times 2 = 16$ $\times 48$
     $3 - 2 = 1$ $7 - 2 = 5$ $14 - 11 = 3$

24 Wildcat

25 D; the two lower circles combine to form the circle
above. Similar symbols disappear.

26 4; $64 \div 8 = 8 - 2 = 6$
    $21 \div 7 = 3 - 1 = 2$
    $30 \div 5 = 6 - 1 = 5$
    $24 \div 4 = 6 - 2 = 4$

27 b) a leg of mutton

28 Minnow

29 Carp, approve

30 D

31 a) food

32 2; the 3 numbers add up to 200.

33 Valorous, fearless

34 Oology

35 2B

36 Man

37 2; there are 2 series:
+1   7, 8, 9, 10
−4   14, 10, 6, 2

38 a) exaltation

39 MATBAN = BANTAM

40 D   x + y = z
1 + 2 = 3
But similar symbols disappear

Test eight

Answers

1 EMRUD = DEMUR

2 2; the numbers in each circle add up to 33.

3 Rainstorm (minor arts)

4 Sistine Chapel; to give: obi, was, eat, own, fee, lac, dip, ode, nil.

5 20 minutes; $30 \times \dfrac{10}{15}$

6 C; the top apex and the bottom right apex are folded over

7 5

8 Defeatist

9 D; the figures outside the square move from the 12 o'clock to the 9 o'clock position. The circle goes in the middle of the square and the other figure half inside the square.

10 Terminal, velocity

11 Crook, cheat

12 Overt

13 26; add 3, 4, 5, 6 then 7

14 A penny for your thoughts

15 Mogul; it is an Indian dynasty. The rest are Chinese.

16 e) words

17 6; in the first circle opposite segments total 7, in the second circle they total 8, and in the third circle 9.

18 SHA; Marsha, Sharon.

19 A; at each stage the black circle moves one segment anti-clockwise, then two segments, then three etc. The white circle does the same, but clockwise.

20 B; A is a mirror image of D and C a mirror image of E.

21 24; $24 + 7 + 6 - 9 = 28$
$9 + 14 + 8 - 4 = 27$
$9 + 16 + 10 - 11 = 24$

22 They all contain boys' names in reverse.
LEN, PAT, RON, TOM, GUS

23 312211; each number describes the previous number, eg three 1s, two 2s, one 1.

24 Ringtail

25 B; the lower two circles combine to form the circle above but similar symbols disappear.

26 Jumpsuit

27 CICADA

28 125; $(11 \times 14) - 26 = 128$
$(9 \times 16) - 18 = 126$
$(17 \times 8) - 11 = 125$

29 d) a fencing stroke

30 C

31 Repudiate, disclaim

32 Peer

33 b) ostentation

34 10; there are two series:
$$-2 \quad 12, 10, 8, 6$$
$$+3 \quad 1, 4, 7, 10$$

35 B; $x + y = z$
$$1 + 2 = 3$$
But similar symbols disappear.

36 d) flesh coloured

37 11; opposite segments reduce by 7, smaller taken from larger.

38 Colossal, gigantic

39 SUMPOS = POSSUM

40 C

Test nine

Answers

1   D; opposite segments are a mirror-image of each other.

2   Ordinary, inspired

3   Esoteric

4   D; black circles turn to white diamonds; white circles turn to black diamonds, and vice versa.

5   1; reading clockwise   89 + 54 = 143
                           98 + 31 = 129
                           84 + 87 = 171

6   Plum pie, plump eye

7   All contain internal anagrams; p(refer)able, purv(eye)d, tara(did)dle, bag(pip)es, bej(ewe)lled.

8   Blessed, cursed

9   A;

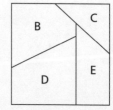

10 B; looking both across and down the contents of the third tile is determined by the contents of the first two tiles. Lines are carried forward except when a line appears in both tiles, in which case it is cancelled out.

11 Elate; the rest are anagram pairs: glean/angle, riled/idler, horse/shore, groan/organ, caned/dance, eager/agree, owned/endow, broth/throb.

12 LAND = 91; nine straight lines, one curved

13 K; start at the bottom left square and travel up and down columns to read 'snakes and ladders'.

14 E; all the rest are the same figure rotated.

15 Indirect, straight

16 Starting-point

17 F

18 161;   68 + 93 = 161

19 Damson; to give: bid, lea, ham, his, too, fan.

20 8; $3 \times 8 = 24 - 6 = 18$

21 a) wooden trellis

22 152; $(9 \times 17) + 18 = 171$
$(8 \times 13) + 16 = 120$
$(11 \times 12) + 20 = 152$

23 Cheetah

24 29; 22 21 30 29 38 37 46
     -1 $+9$ -1 $+9$ -1 $+9$

25 A

26 Paravane

27 Corporeal, spiritual

28 e) a sea monster

29 $1\dfrac{12}{13}$; $\dfrac{3}{5} \times \dfrac{125}{39} = \dfrac{25}{13} = 1\dfrac{12}{13}$

30 E; the lower two circles combine to form the circle
     above but similar symbols disappear.

31 Tootle

32 -1; there are two series:
     $+2\frac{1}{2}$ 6, 8½, 11, 13½
     -4 11, 7, 3, -1

33 c) fall

34 Badger

35 A

36 Phantoms, spectres

37 i or j

38 e) wind

39 2420484; 1, 2, 4, 8, 16, 32, 64, 128, 256, 512, 1024, 2048, 4096

40 F; A is the same as G
C is the same as E
B is the same as D

Test ten

Answers

1 5246; in the others the middle number is half of the number formed by the first and last digits, eg 3186 (36/2 = 18).

2 Circumvent

3 C; the figure at the bottom goes to the top. The figure inside the larger figure at the bottom rotates through 90° and goes to the top. The larger figure at the bottom reduces in size and goes inside the figure now at the top.

4 Eradicate, eliminate

5 Eternity ring

6 C; it contains the black dot and one smaller white circle inside the large circle, and one smaller white circle and black circle partly inside the large circle.

7 Charmingly

8 B; the smallest number is discarded at each stage and the remaining numbers travel in the opposite direction to the previous stage.

9 E; so one dot is in one circle and the other dot is in the circle and ellipse.

10 2; 7 + 8 +8 = 23

11 Eventful, ordinary

12 117; alternately subtract, then add the sum of the digits of the previous number.

13 A; the triangles become one large triangle and the truncated ellipse becomes two, rotating 180° and going inside the triangle.

14 Sleigh ride

15 Loom

16 Chivalrous

17 C; at each stage one of the sections goes through 45° and continues to move 45° at subsequent stages.

18 6; add 0.5, 1, 1.5, 2

19 DEPNU = UPEND

20 Take the top circle on the left with the bottom circle on the right, etc, to spell out beard, heard, heart, learn, pearl, weary and yearn, with the addition of EAR.

21 Cashmere

22 c) strychnine

23 b) ventage = a small hole in a flute.

24 b) a dance

25 E; B is the same as F
    A is the same as D
    C is the same as G

26 c) marriageable

27 Boxer

28 a) paddling

29 Pippin

30 C; the two lower circles combine to form the circle
   above but similar symbols disappear.

31 364;   the sequence is × 3 + 1.

32 Bearing, mien

33 Gibbons

34 91; starting with 100 reduce by nine each segment,
   jumping three clockwise.

35 A

36 7½;   there are two series:
        +3½   4, 7 ½, 11, 14½
        −1½   12, 10½, 9, 7½

37 Feminine, womanish

38 Ounce

39 Ant

40 C; the lower two circles combine to form the circle
   above but similar symbols disappear.